The
American Medical Association

BOOK OF
BACK CARE

The American Medical Association
Home Health Library

The
American Medical Association

BOOK OF
BACK CARE

Developed by the
American Medical Association

MEDICAL ADVISORS

William F. Donaldson, Jr., M.D.
Norman W. Hoover, M.D.

Written by Marion Steinmann
Illustrations by Mark Rosenthal

RANDOM HOUSE   NEW YORK

The recommendations and information contained in this book are appropriate in most cases. For specific information concerning a personal medical condition, however, the AMA suggests that you see a physician.

The names of organizations appearing in this book are given for informational purposes only. Their inclusion implies neither approval nor disapproval by AMA.

Library of Congress Cataloging in Publication Data
Steinmann, Marion.
The American Medical Association book of backcare.
Includes index.
1. Backache. 2. Back—Care and hygiene. I. American
Medical Association. II. Title.
RD768.S734   617'.56   81–48298
ISBN 0–394–51038–0   AACR2

Manufactured in the United States of America
24689753
First Edition

MEDICAL ADVISORS

William F. Donaldson, Jr., M.D., is a past president of the American Academy of Orthopaedic Surgeons and is a current member of the Board of Regents of the American College of Surgeons. In addition, he is medical director of Children's Hospital of Pittsburgh. Dr. Donaldson serves as chairman of the Board of Trustees of the *Journal of Bone and Joint Surgery* and as president of A.C.O.R.E., the Advisory Council for Orthopaedic Resident Education. He received his M.D. degree from the University of Pittsburgh School of Medicine. Dr. Donaldson is in private practice in Pittsburgh. He is married and has four grown children.

Norman W. Hoover, M.D., is a diplomate of the American Board of Orthopedic Surgery and a former staff member of the Mayo Clinic in Rochester, Minnesota. He has been director of the American Medical Association's Department of International Medicine and has studied infectious diseases of the spine during six years at the University of Saigon. Dr. Hoover is a member of the American Academy of Orthopaedic Surgeons and the American College of Surgeons. He received his M.D. degree from the University of Minnesota Medical School and is in private practice in Mason City, Iowa. Dr. Hoover is married and has four children.

PREFACE

Surely the most valuable asset we Americans have, both as individuals and as a nation, is our health. Good health is the cornerstone of almost every productive human activity. Yet all too often we squander our health, either by neglecting our physical and emotional needs or by indulging in habits that are patently harmful.

In recent decades our failure to maintain adequately our health has been largely obscured by the fanfare surrounding the introduction of a host of new "wonder drugs" and an imposing array of advanced medical technology. But these innovations, despite the many benefits they have brought us, are not adequate by themselves to meet our health needs and aspirations. Something more is required—something important.

It is now clear beyond doubt that if we wish to enjoy the attributes of continued good health in the years ahead, the impetus will have to come from each of us, working as individuals in our own best interests. As individuals, each of us is better qualified than anyone else to act as the guardian of his or her health. By looking within ourselves and adopting prudent health habits and sensible lifestyles, we can prevent unnecessary illness, needless loss of vitality, and premature old age or death.

There is, moreover, a special economic urgency about all this, an urgency that affects every one of us. Inflation has pushed medical costs—and family medical bills—to unprecedented levels. Certainly one of the most effective ways the individual can combat this numbing inflation is to avoid the avoidable and prevent the preventable.

These are the reasons that have motivated the American Medical Association, in collaboration with Random House, to publish this book. It is one of a series of books, to be collectively entitled the *American Medical Association Home Health Library,* which will bring you the latest, most authoritative and most useful information on a wide range of health-care subjects. As doctors, we firmly believe that if you are given the facts, and the professional guidance necessary to understand and apply those facts, you will act wisely in your own behalf.

An estimated seven million Americans are currently undergoing treatment for chronic back problems. Roughly two million new cases are being added to patient rolls each year. Back injuries are said to account for 25 percent of all disability payments.

And yet much of this suffering could be alleviated. If people took care of their backs—if they got the proper exercise and avoided the foolish habits that place undue stress on the human back—they would spare themselves a great deal of pain and expense.

This is where knowledge can play a key role. Even in cases where injury or disease has already occurred, you will be better equipped to work with your doctor toward a solution if you have a basic understanding of how your back is structured, how it functions and what your particular problem is.

The practice of medicine is of course an art as well as a science, and it is thus susceptible to varying opinions regarding the exact procedures that should be followed in any individual case. Nonetheless, we are confident that the information in this book reflects the highest standards of scientific accuracy.

Let me add just one final thought: We look upon this book as an important opportunity to talk directly with you, the individual consumer of health- and medical-care services. We believe that once you are equipped with sound and balanced information, you will be able to shape a better, more fruitful life for yourself and those closest to you. That is certainly our hope.

James H. Sammons, M.D.
Executive Vice President
American Medical Association

ACKNOWLEDGMENTS

The publication of *BackCare* would not have been possible without the generous help of the many men and women who contributed their time and expertise to the book's preparation.

In addition to Drs. William F. Donaldson, Jr., and Norman W. Hoover, whose scientific knowledge and dedication to excellence have been invaluable, we wish to thank the following individuals and organizations: Alice Haywood (Hyattsville, Maryland); W. H. Kirkaldy-Willis, M.D. (Saskatoon, Saskatchewan, Canada); Alf L. Nachemson, M.D. (Göteborg, Sweden); Albert B. Schultz, Ph.D. (Chicago, Illinois); Carolyn M. Scott (Philadelphia, Pennsylvania); Solomon Sobel, M.D. (Rockville, Maryland); Ian Tattersall, Ph.D. (New York, New York); Eric J. Trotter, D.V.M. (Ithaca, New York); Leon L. Wiltse, M.D. (Long Beach, California); James M. Yonts (Chicago, Illinois); Marianne Zachrisson-Forssell (Jönköping, Sweden). Also the National Institute on Aging (Robert N. Butler, M.D., Director) and the National Institute of Arthritis, Diabetes, and Digestive and Kidney Diseases (G. Donald Whedon, M.D., Director).

To Charles A. Wimpfheimer, Klara Glowczewski and Bernard Klein of Random House for their knowledgeable guidance and support.

We also wish to express our gratitude to the following members of AMA's editorial team for their creativity, skill and insistence on high quality: Marion Steinmann, Mark Rosenthal, Kathleen A. Kaye, Carole A. Fina, Ralph L. Linnenburger, David LaHoda, Sophie Klim, and Patricia Evilsizer and Micaela Sullivan of the AMA Division of Library and Archival Sciences.

Finally, we want to thank the men and women with back problems who so graciously shared their experiences with us and with the readers of this book. We promised these people that in order to protect their privacy we would not use their names, but their contribution to this book has been significant, and we are very grateful to them.

Charles C. Renshaw, Jr.
Editorial Director
American Medical Association
Consumer Book Program

CONTENTS

LIST OF ILLUSTRATIONS

The
American Medical Association

BOOK OF
BACK CARE

INTRODUCTION: THE SCOPE OF THE PROBLEM

An aching back is one of the most common afflictions of humankind, so common that it is almost part of the human condition. Most of us, at some time in our lives, suffer from backache.

- According to the National Center for Health Statistics' National Ambulatory Medical Care Survey, American men and women, in a recent year, paid 16,610,000 visits to physicians' offices for back and neck symptoms. This was the second most common reason for visiting a doctor (throat symptoms being the most common).
- Studies conducted by M. Laurens Rowe, M.D., an orthopedic surgeon in Rochester, New York, found a similarly high prevalence of back trouble. Records of 237 men in their early sixties (on the eve of their retirement from the Eastman Kodak Company) showed that 56 percent had at some time during their career experienced back pain severe enough to need medical treatment. About half of these men had experienced backaches bad enough to require time off from work.
- Backaches were second only to upper respiratory infections in causing absences from work, according to another study at Eastman Kodak conducted by Dr. Rowe. In one 2,000-man operating division over a ten-year period, the time loss from work due to low back problems averaged four hours per man per year. (The amount of

time lost from upper respiratory infections averaged eight hours per man per year.)

• In studies conducted by Lennart Hult of the Karolinska Institute in Stockholm, Sweden, 60 percent of a group of 1,137 men, from diverse occupations, had at some point experienced symptoms of back trouble, ranging from fatigue to sudden incapacitating pain. In 36 percent, the backaches had been severe enough that the men had lost time from work. In a related study in the small town of Munkfors in western Sweden, even more people had had back trouble; 80 percent of a group of 276 men in heavy occupations (ironworkers, timber cutters) had back problems.

• "Sometime during our active lives 80 percent of us will experience back pain to some extent," concludes Alf L. Nachemson, M.D., professor and chairman of the Department of Orthopaedic Surgery at Sahlgren Hospital, University of Göteborg, Sweden, and a noted scientific researcher in back problems. "Men are afflicted as often as women, white-collar workers as often as blue-collar workers."

• "Worldwide, during the next decade," Dr. Nachemson calculates, "there will be about 2 billion patients suffering from low back pain."

Backaches, common as they are, very rarely kill us, but as the statistics show, they cause an uncommon amount of misery. Back problems have afflicted human beings since the beginning of the species; many of them—as we will see throughout this book—are part of our inborn biological heritage. Most back trouble, moreover, cannot be completely cured, in the sense of permanently eradicating the cause of the problem. Back problems are thus usually chronic diseases—that is, they tend to persist for years, even decades, flaring up from time to time, often for no apparent reason, and then spontaneously and just as mysteriously subsiding again. Because back troubles tend to occur during a person's adult years, these recurrent attacks of pain can interfere with the prime years of life.

Fortunately, however, most people do not have severe back trouble. The overwhelming majority do not need surgery, and for the few who do, it usually solves the problem. While physicians do not have quick cures for most back problems, they do have a sizable array of treatments to alleviate the symptoms for most people. As will be pointed out throughout this book, many of the most effective ways to prevent backaches involve things that no doctor can do for us but that only we, as we go about our daily lives, can do for ourselves.

To help you use this book, here is an outline of the chapters:

The back is an extraordinarily complex structure made up of bones, cartilage, nerves, blood vessels, ligaments, and layers upon layers of muscle, each with its own potential for causing trouble. Chapter 1 describes, in illustrations and text, the basic anatomy of the back while introducing some necessary medical terminology. It also explains what happens within the back as we bend and twist.

Chapter 2 explains how the anatomy of the back changes throughout life. Scarcely have the bones reached their full growth than other parts of the back begin deteriorating. Many of these normal changes with age contribute significantly to back troubles.

Chapter 3 describes—again in both illustrations and text—the many diseases that can affect the back. Because some of these diseases can be serious and should be treated promptly, and also because there are many diseases of other parts of the body that can first show up as back pain, it is important—if you have persistent backache—to consult a physician to find out the cause.

Chapter 4 discusses the many kinds of treatments available for back problems. This chapter also tells you the kinds of physicians who treat back disease, when you should see a doctor—that is, the danger signs that should prompt you to consult a physician—and the methods doctors use to diagnose back disease.

Chapter 5 shows, again in illustrations and text, many practical measures all of us can take to minimize the strain on the back and to help prevent backaches.

Chapter 6 explores the provocative question of whether our unique posture is the cause of our human propensity toward back trouble. The chapter looks at how the major design features of the back have evolved over the last half billion or so years, and also at how human backs compare with those of other animals today—the features we share with other animals and the features that are ours alone.

All of the people whom you will meet in this book are real people with real back problems. We have, however, changed their names in order to preserve their privacy.

Many parts of the back and many back diseases have names unfamiliar to the general reader, so in addition to defining these terms in the body of the text, we have included a glossary of the most important medical words.

Besides helping you decide when to consult a doctor about a back problem, this book should also assist you in understanding what he or she may tell you. It is *not*, however, designed to replace your doctor; no book can do that. If anything you read within these pages seems different from what your doctor says, pay attention to your doctor; only he or she is in a position to know the details of your particular case.

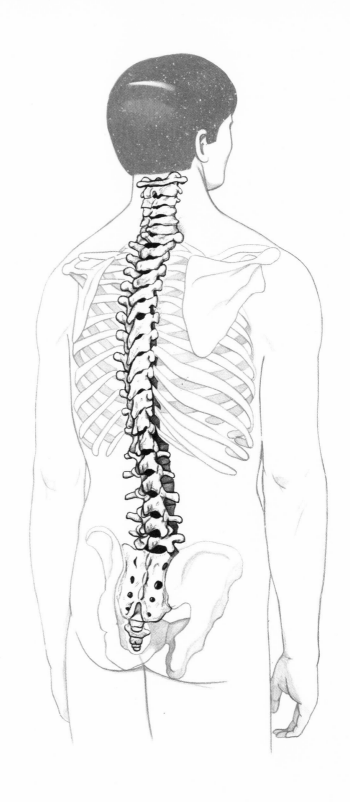

1

A GUIDED TOUR
OF THE
HUMAN BACK

In contrast to such hidden organs as the brain and the heart, the back is an observable part of the body. We can see it in a mirror and we can touch it with our fingers. Yet concealed beneath the surface is a structure of extraordinary complexity consisting not only of dozens of overlapping bones (see the illustration opposite) connected to still other bones (shown in rust in the illustration) but also of numerous other, softer tissues: cartilage, blood vessels, nerves, ligaments and muscles. Before we can understand what can go wrong with the back, we need to know more about how the back is built and how it works. Let's begin our tour of the uniquely human upright back by taking a close look at its basic building block.

The Vertebra

The basic building block of the spine is a bone—the *vertebra*—of a relatively modest dimension: no wider than a few inches. Yet the human vertebra has been sculpted by hundreds of millions of years of evolution into an astonishingly intricate three-dimensional shape that performs four key jobs within the back.

The main part of the vertebra is its body, which is roughly cylindrical in shape. (In the illustration on page 10, we are looking at a typical vertebra from the side and slightly above.) When the many vertebrae are stacked one atop the next, their bodies form a vertical

column that supports the weight of the upper part of the body
against the steady downward pull of gravity—just as a column
supports the weight of a building. To the rear of the body of the
vertebra is a sizable vertical hole. When the vertebrae are stacked,
these holes line up to form a vertical tunnel, the *spinal canal,* which
encloses and protects the delicate *spinal cord* (indicated schemati-
cally in rust).

Behind the spinal canal, no less than seven different bony projections, or processes, jut from each vertebra. (In anatomical terms the
word "process" means a part of a structure that projects outward.
The processes are best seen in the illustration opposite. Here the
same vertebra has been turned nearly 90 degrees, so that we are now
looking at it from the rear.) Four of these fingerlike processes form
joints or articulations with other vertebrae and are therefore called
articular processes. The upper pair of projections are the *superior
articular processes;* the lower pair, the *inferior articular processes.*

The remaining three projections—the *spinous process,* to the rear,
and the two *transverse processes,* one to either side—are all levers.
The back muscles are attached to these processes, and as the muscles
contract and relax, they pull and release these levers to bend and
twist the spine. (The word "vertebra" comes from the Latin *vertere,*

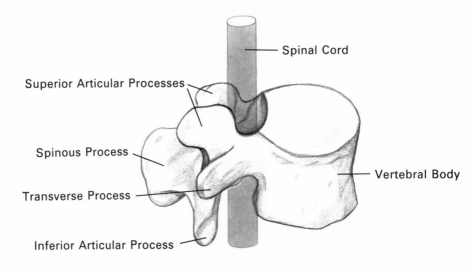

Spinal Cord

Superior Articular Processes

Spinous Process

Transverse Process

Inferior Articular Process

Vertebral Body

A VERTEBRA, SIDE VIEW

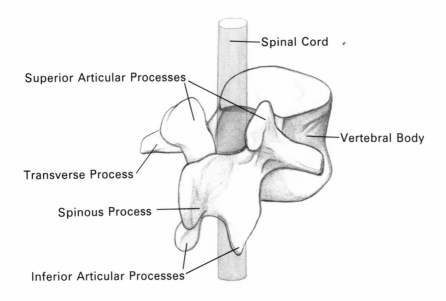

Spinal Cord

Superior Articular Processes

Vertebral Body

Transverse Process

Spinous Process

Inferior Articular Processes

A VERTEBRA, REAR VIEW

meaning to turn.) The spinous processes also are the most readily accessible part of the spine; they are what we can feel when we run our fingers up and down the backbone.

The Disc

The other basic component of the spine is the *intervertebral disc,* a cylindrical pad the same diameter as the vertebral body but not nearly so thick. The disc is made, however, of far different material: a softer, slightly yellowish substance called fibrocartilage, which is similar to the cartilage forming the nose and ears.

The disc also is far simpler in structure than the vertebra; it has two main parts. The central portion is a pulpy, jellylike mass called the *nucleus pulposus.* Encircling the nucleus are layers of parallel fibers that hold the nucleus in place. This outer portion of the disc is called the *annulus fibrosus* (Latin for fibrous ring). For greater strength, fibers in each layer of the annulus run in different directions (see the illustration on page 12). There actually is no sharp demarcation between these two parts of the disc; the nucleus blends imperceptibly into the annulus.

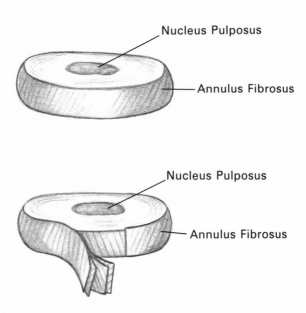

Nucleus Pulposus

Annulus Fibrosus

Nucleus Pulposus

Annulus Fibrosus

A DISC

The disc is thus constructed something like an automobile tire, and like a tire has a high internal pressure of its own. While a tire's pressure comes from compressed air, the disc's pressure is due to water. Discs are over 80 percent water. The disc's high water content makes it highly elastic—that is, able to change its shape and then return to its original form. This gives the spine flexibility; without discs, we would be unable to bend and twist as readily as we do. The disc's high water content also enables it to absorb any jolts or blows to the spine. The disc is, in fact, one of the body's chief shock absorbers.

The disc is also a common source of back trouble, as we will discuss later. Among other things, it sometimes can even, like an automobile tire, have a blowout.

How the Vertebrae Join

Each typical pair of vertebrae in the spine is both separated and joined together by a disc, which fits neatly—like the meat in a sandwich—between the two vertebral bodies (see the illustrations below and on the next page). This *disc joint* is the primary weight-bearing joint of the back. At this joint, the bony vertebrae and the cartilaginous disc are so intimately bonded together that in normal circumstances no motion is possible between them. Our ability to bend and twist the spine is entirely due to the elastic nature of the disc material.

Each pair of vertebrae is also joined together at the rear by two secondary joints. The two fingerlike inferior articular processes of the upper vertebra reach down to overlap the lower vertebra and fit snugly between the two superior articular processes of this lower vertebra. The interlocking of the inferior and superior articular processes substantially buttresses the spinal joints and stiffens the

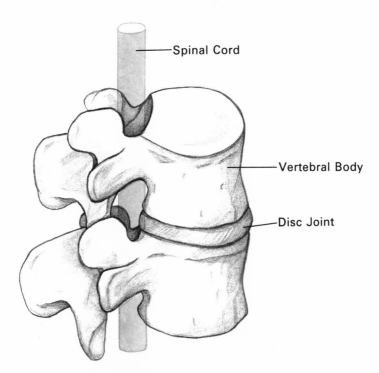

Spinal Cord

Vertebral Body

Disc Joint

THE VERTEBRAL JOINTS, SIDE VIEW

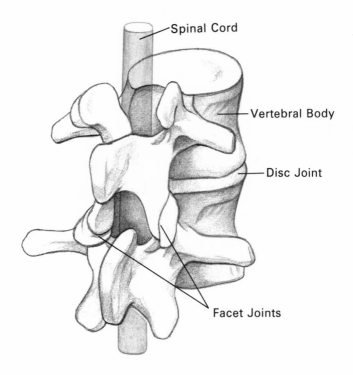

THE VERTEBRAL JOINTS, REAR VIEW

spinal column. (This ingenious interlocking mechanism evolved several hundred million years ago as our early vertebrate ancestors crawled out of the sea and began living on the land. When their spines were no longer supported by water, they had to develop stiffer backbones.)

The articular processes join together along small flat surfaces something like the facets that cause a diamond to sparkle. These small rear joints are thus known as the *facet joints*. Doctors also often call them the apophyseal joints, or simply the posterior joints. The flat surfaces of the facet joints glide over each other to some extent and allow some motion, but they largely serve to limit how far we can bend and twist the back.

Each pair of vertebrae are thus connected together by three separate joints: the main disc joint and the two auxiliary facet joints at the rear. Any one or combination of these three joints can be a source of back problems.

Special Vertebrae

While each of the vertebrae follows the same basic plan—a body, an opening for the spinal cord, and seven processes for joints and muscle attachments—each is also subtly different. No two vertebrae are shaped precisely the same way. The most eccentric of them are the vertebrae at the very top and very bottom of the spinal column.

The top two vertebrae in the neck (see the illustration below) are specially modified to join the spine to the head and also to permit the motions of the head. The uppermost vertebra has no vertebral

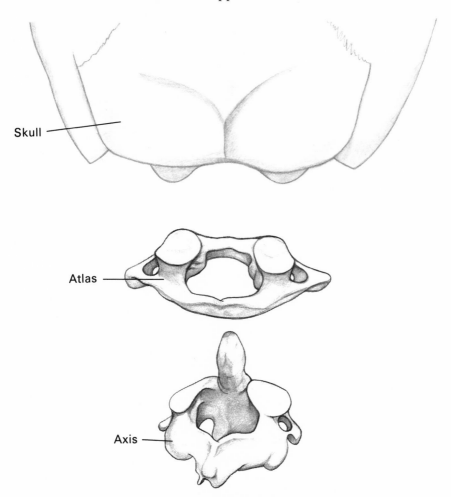

Skull

Atlas

Axis

THE TOP NECK VERTEBRAE, REAR VIEW

body at all, consisting instead of an enormously enlarged central hole with two saucerlike surfaces on either side to support the skull. This topmost vertebra is called the *atlas* after the giant in Greek mythology who supports the world on his shoulders. When we nod the head yes, we are rocking the bones of the skull on the atlas. The second vertebra, called the *axis,* has a sizable post projecting upward at the front that fits neatly into the wide ringlike opening in the atlas. When we shake the head no, we are swiveling the atlas around this post on the axis. (In the illustration, the skull, atlas and axis are separated so they can be seen clearly. In the body, they fit closely together.)

The seventh and last vertebra in the neck (see the illustration below) has an unusually long *spinous process* projecting horizontally toward the rear. This forms the pronounced bump we see and feel at the base of the neck.

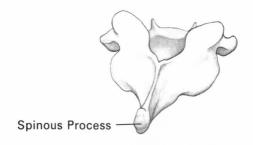

Spinous Process ———

THE LOWEST NECK VERTEBRA, REAR VIEW

At the bottom of the spinal column are two odd-shaped bones: the *sacrum* and the *coccyx.* In the illustration opposite we are looking at the sacrum and coccyx from the side and from slightly above. In the illustration on page 18, these bones have been turned nearly 90 degrees, so that we are now looking at them from the rear. The sacrum is the largest bone in the spine, measuring several inches or more in both length and breadth. Its great size befits its role as the base or pedestal of the spinal column, where it bears the concentrated weight of the entire upper half of the body. The sacrum's size and importance may be the reason for its name, which derives from ancient Latin and Greek and means sacred bone or mighty bone, the latter apparently a reference to its imposing size and position. (Another theory is that the ancients considered the bone sacred because they used it in sacrifices of some sort.) The sacrum is formed by the fusion during our growing years of five individual vertebrae. This accounts for its strange wedgelike shape, its many bumps and ridges (which correspond to the projecting vertebral processes) and its many holes (corresponding to the spaces between the vertebrae).

Dangling below the sacrum like an afterthought is the tiny vestigial tailbone, or coccyx. The name coccyx comes from the Greek word for cuckoo; presumably someone once fancied that the bone resembled a cuckoo's beak. Like the sacrum, the coccyx is formed

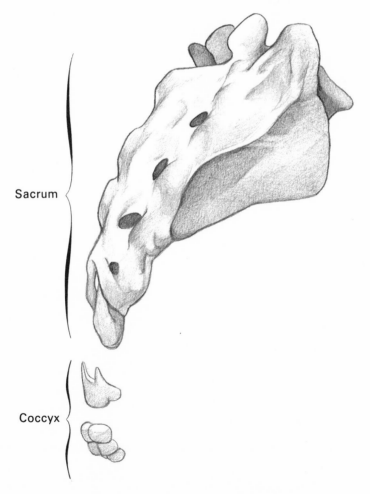

Sacrum

Coccyx

THE SACRUM AND COCCYX, SIDE VIEW

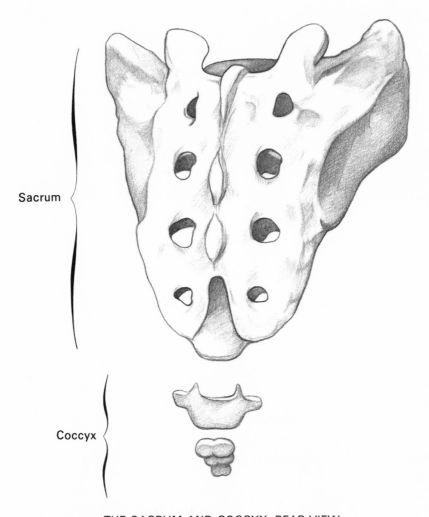

Sacrum

Coccyx

THE SACRUM AND COCCYX, REAR VIEW

by the fusion of, usually, four rudimentary vertebrae. These rudimentary vertebrae may be entirely fused or they may be only partially fused, so that the coccyx is in two pieces, as shown here. (Again, in the illustrations, the sacrum and the two pieces of the coccyx are separated. In the body, they are joined closely together.) While the coccyx no longer has a tail to wag and plays no role in supporting the body, it is not totally useless. The big buttocks muscle, the gluteus maximus, one of the most powerful in the body, is partially attached to the coccyx and uses it as a purchase for moving the legs.

The Spinal Column

The total number of vertebrae we have in the spine varies according to how we count them. As you can see in the illustration on page 20, we have twenty-four individual vertebrae above the sacrum. If we count the sacrum and coccyx as a single bone each, we have twenty-six bones in the back. However, if we count the sacrum as the five vertebrae it actually is and also count the coccyx as four vertebrae, then we have a total of thirty-three vertebrae in the spinal column. All of the bones that form the spine are also collectively called the *backbone.*

In the body, these vertebrae are stacked one on top of another, with a disc between each pair of vertebral bodies, to form an upright spinal column—a spine unique in the animal kingdom. Looking at the human spine directly from the front, we see the stacked cylindrical vertebral bodies with the transverse processes extending out on either side like wings. We can also see that the backbone as a whole is symmetrical and essentially straight. It extends from high up in the neck behind the face, where the atlas lies just below the level of the ears and nose (the atlas is about in line with where a mustache would be and is not unlike one in shape), down well into the hips, where the lowermost individual vertebra, sacrum and coccyx are all below the top of the hipbones. The bones of the spine are connected to each other and to other bones (shown in rust in the illustration) by a total of about a hundred and three separate joints. There are seventy-six facet and disc joints connecting vertebrae to other vertebrae, plus twenty-four joints connecting vertebrae to ribs, two joints connecting the sacrum to the hipbones, and one joint connecting the atlas to the skull.

In women, the sacrum and the hipbones are somewhat wider than in men, but there are no other known significant differences between male and female spines.

Physicians divide the spinal column into several distinct regions. The top seven are called the *cervical* (neck) *vertebrae;* these are the smallest and most delicate, since they bear only the weight of the head. The next twelve are the *thoracic* (chest) *vertebrae;* these are considerably larger because they must carry the additional weight of the shoulders and arms. The thoracic vertebrae are also specially shaped to form joints with the ribs.

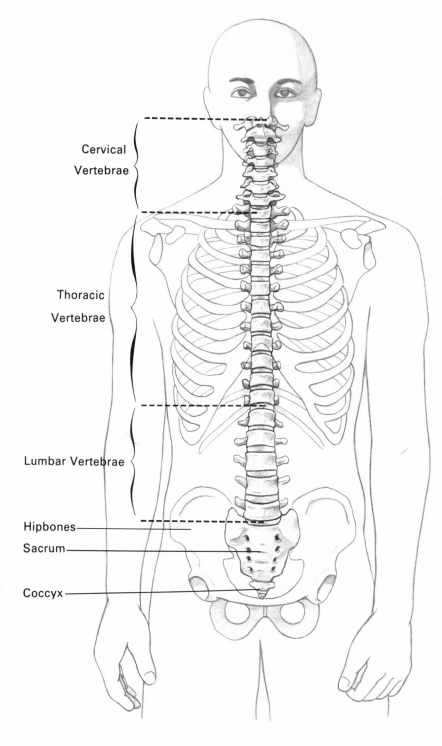

Cervical
Vertebrae

Thoracic
Vertebrae

Lumbar Vertebrae

Hipbones

Sacrum

Coccyx

THE SPINAL COLUMN, FRONT VIEW

The next five vertebrae in the lower portion of the spine are the *lumbar vertebrae*. (The word "lumbar" means "pertaining to the loins," the part of the body between the ribs and hipbones.) The lumbar vertebrae are the largest of the individual vertebrae—with the bottommost one the most massive of the five—since they must bear the most weight. This lumbar area is also the region of the spine most subject to back disease, a susceptibility partially due to the weight load on this part of the spine. Below the lumbar region the sacrum is firmly seated within the encircling hipbones, while the tiny coccyx dangles below it.

Most of the backbone's length is due to the vertebrae; the discs usually contribute only about a quarter of its height above the sacrum. The discs are so elastic, however, that they compress measurably during the day due to the weight of the body. When we go to bed at night, we are actually a half to three-quarters of an inch shorter than we are when we get up in the morning. As we lie in bed during the night, the discs are largely relieved of pressure and regain their former height. If the discs are totally relieved of the body's weight for longer periods of time, as happens in space, they will expand even more in height. This effect was measured during the mid-1970s in the course of the fourth American Skylab Mission, when three astronauts spent eighty-four days orbiting the earth. The largest gain in height was made by Pilot William R. Pogue, who "grew" some two inches. By the time he returned to the earth's surface, however, gravity had reduced him to his normal preflight height.

The Spinal Curves

When viewed from the side (see the illustration on page 22), the spinal column appears very different than it does from the front. From this perspective the spine is not symmetrical; we see stacked cylindrical vertebral bodies on the front of the column and interlocking facet joints on the rear. But even more striking, we can see that the spine is also not at all straight but curves forward and backward. From the atlas, just beneath the ear, the neck curves forward in a gentle *cervical curve*. Then, from just below the prominent vertebrae at the base of the neck, the spine sweeps backward

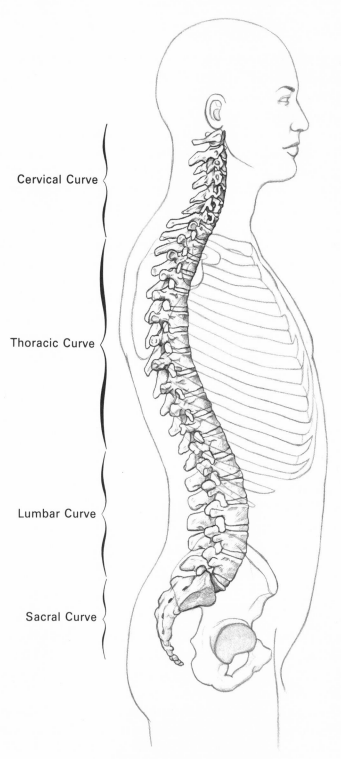

Cervical Curve

Thoracic Curve

Lumbar Curve

Sacral Curve

THE SPINAL COLUMN, SIDE VIEW

in a long *thoracic curve*. From about the level of the bottom of the ribs, it curves forward again in a more marked *lumbar curve*. And finally the sacrum and coccyx themselves angle sharply backward in the *sacral curve*.

These four curves are another unique feature of the human spinal column. No other animal has such curves in its spine, not even our closest primate relatives, the great apes. And humans are not born with these curves. They develop in the spine during childhood as we first sit up and walk about.

These curves probably make the spine more flexible up and down, thus providing another shock absorber for protecting the brain. "If you have a curved rod and press down on it, it bends more easily than a straight rod would," explains Albert B. Schultz, Ph.D., an engineer at the University of Illinois at Chicago Circle who for many years has studied the human spine as a mechanical structure. "When you bang down on your heels and come flat on your feet, that shock travels up your spine. If your spine is curved, it absorbs the shock better."

One consequence of these complex curves in the backbone is the curious fact that most of the vertebrae do not, as one would expect, lie horizontally to the ground. Only at the centers of the cervical, thoracic and lumbar curves are the vertebrae and their discs horizontal. One might also expect that the column as a whole would stand firmly on a horizontal surface. It does not. The sacrum, the pedestal of our spine, tilts so sharply that its upper surface slopes nearly 45 degrees. This steep slope of the sacrum is a factor in one type of back disease, spondylolisthesis (see page 86).

The Nerves

As mentioned earlier, a typical vertebra has a sizable hole in it just behind its body. When the vertebrae are stacked, these holes line up to form the spinal canal, which extends the full length of the spinal column. The spinal cord runs vertically from the base of the brain through this bony channel.

A delicate bundle of nerve cells and fibers about the diameter of the little finger, the spinal cord is the main line of communication between the brain and the rest of the body. Whenever the brain receives a message from the body or sends out a command to it, the

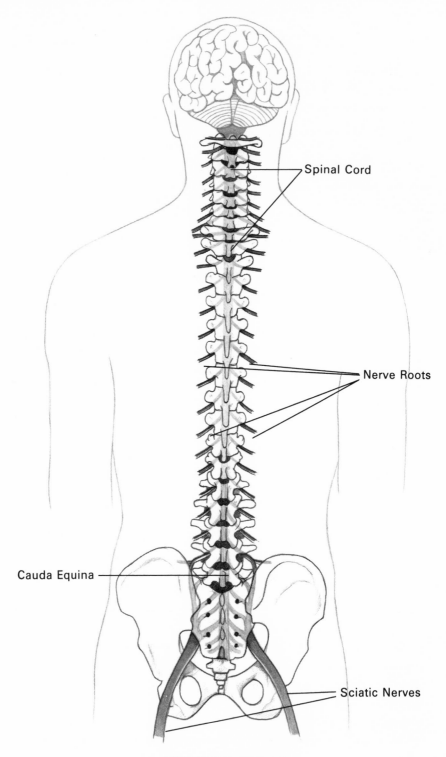

Spinal Cord

Nerve Roots

Cauda Equina

Sciatic Nerves

THE SPINAL NERVES

message travels, in the form of an electrochemical signal, along these nerve fibers in the spinal cord. Housing and thus protecting this crucial link between brain and body is, as mentioned earlier, one of the spinal column's several important jobs.

The spinal cord branches at regular intervals, sending off smaller bundles of nerves in pairs, one on either side, from between each pair of vertebrae. These nerve bundles service different levels of the body. The portions of these secondary nerve bundles that emerge from the spinal column are called *nerve roots.* We have thirty-one pairs of these nerve roots, sixty-two altogether, emerging from the spine. In the illustration opposite, we are looking at the spine from the rear. The brain, spinal cord and nerve roots are shown in rust, while the spinal column and hipbones are in black. The nerve roots are shown as if they had been cut off a short distance from the spine. Beyond this area the nerves combine and recombine, branch and rebranch, to form a neural network of bewildering complexity.

Each pair of nerve roots services a specific part of the body. The pair of nerves emerging from between the fourth and fifth neck vertebrae, for instance, activates muscles that help move the shoulders. The nerves coming out from between the sixth and seventh neck vertebrae run to muscles serving the wrists and fingers. In the lower spine, nerves that exit from between the fourth and fifth lumbar vertebrae go to muscles moving the hips and knees, while those emerging from between the fifth lumbar vertebra and the sacrum activate our feet.

Curiously, the spinal cord itself terminates well short of the end of the spinal canal, tapering off several inches above the waist. Below this area, individual nerve fibers continue to run downward through the spinal canal in parallel vertical strands somewhat resembling a horse's tail. Physicians therefore call them our *cauda equina* (see the illustration), Latin for horse's tail. Thus while the human species has no external tail, we do have two internal tails of sorts: the coccyx and this hidden tail of nerves.

Several of the nerves that leave the spinal column in the lumbar area combine near the hips with nerves that exit through holes in the sacrum to form a single thick nerve, one on either side of the body, called the *sciatic nerve* (see the illustration). ("Sciatic" comes from the Latin word for hip.) This is the largest nerve in the body.

Many types of back disease can irritate the roots of the sciatic nerve, causing a distinctive type of pain known as *sciatica*.

In the close-up illustration below, we are again looking at a pair of vertebrae, with a disc sandwiched between their bodies. Notice that the two vertebrae have a considerable opening between them at the side, behind the bodies yet in front of the many vertebral processes. It is through this opening, which physicians call the *intervertebral foramen,* that the root of each spinal nerve (shown in rust), branching off from the spinal cord (also in rust), emerges from the spine. (The nerve roots are also shown as if cut off a short distance from the spine.)

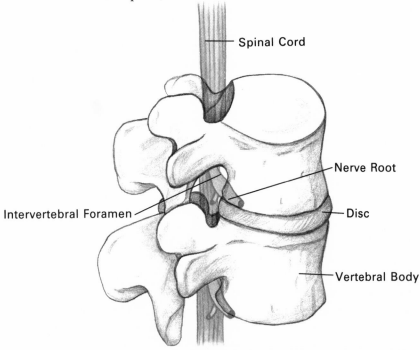

Spinal Cord

Nerve Root

Intervertebral Foramen

Disc

Vertebral Body

THE NERVE ROOTS

This intimate anatomical relationship between the vertebrae, on the one hand, and the spinal cord and nerve roots on the other means that many types of back disease can interfere with the normal functioning of the nervous system. Diseased disc, bone or other spinal tissue can press on or stretch a nerve root. This may produce pain right at that spot in the back, or it may cause pain to shoot out along the course of the afflicted nerve toward some other part of the body —often the legs. Such pressure or stretching may interrupt nerve signals conveying sensations *from* a distant part of the body—a foot, for example. This will cause the foot to feel numb. Or the pressure may interrupt nerve signals conveying commands *to* a distant muscle—again, say, a foot. This will cause weakness in the affected foot muscle. Such muscular weakness, which may be either transient or permanent, may be so subtle that the person is unaware of it. In very severe cases, if diseased tissue compresses or severs the spinal cord, this can cause partial or, more rarely, even complete paralysis.

The Ligaments

An architect designs the supporting column of a building in such a way that the weight-bearing surfaces of its component building blocks lie horizontally to the ground, so that the downward pull of gravity helps stabilize the column by holding each building block firmly upon the block below. The spinal column, oddly, is *not* designed in this way. As mentioned earlier, because of the spine's four curves, most of its building blocks—the vertebrae—do *not* lie horizontally to the ground but are tipped at a decided angle. If the backbone did not have additional support, it would not be stable. Gravity would simply cause it to topple over. The additional support necessary to hold the spinal column upright comes from both the ligaments and the muscles.

Ligaments are tough, elastic bands that bind the bones together and reinforce the joints. In the illustration on page 28 we are looking at part of the spinal column from the side. This view shows some of the major ligaments that strengthen the spine. (Ligaments are shown in rust, while vertebrae and discs are shown in black.) One long ligament, the *anterior longitudinal ligament,* runs like a strip of sturdy tape over the vertebral bodies and discs in front, the full length of the spine, and reinforces the disc joints. A second long ligament, the *posterior longitudinal ligament* (not shown in the illustration), runs the length of the spine over the rear of the vertebral bodies and discs, within the spinal canal, and further strengthens the disc joints. Other short ligaments also reinforce each of the secondary facet joints at the rear of the spinal column. Still other ligaments

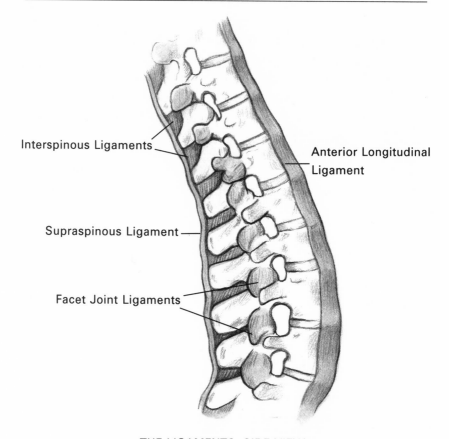

THE LIGAMENTS, SIDE VIEW

Interspinous Ligaments

Anterior Longitudinal Ligament

Supraspinous Ligament

Facet Joint Ligaments

bind together the various processes at the back of the vertebrae. The *intertransverse ligaments* (not shown) connect each transverse process to the next, and the *interspinous* and *supraspinous ligaments* join the spinous processes. Another set of ligaments, the *flaval ligaments* (not visible here), also help bind the rear portions of the vertebrae to each other.

The Muscles

The muscles, of course, are the body tissues that enable us to move through space. We send out signals along nerve fibers commanding the muscles to contract. When they do so, they pull the skeleton from one place to another. By contracting some muscles and relaxing others, we can bend and twist the spinal column.

The muscles also perform a second important job for the spinal column. While the ligaments help bind the vertebrae and discs together, the muscles do most of the work of supporting the spine upright. Without the active work of the muscles, we would be unable either to stand or sit erect. We would simply fall over. A person whose muscles are paralyzed cannot even sit up without assistance.

To understand how the muscles both move and support the spinal column, let us first look at the muscles at the rear of the spine. Here at the back of the back, so to speak, we have an enormous number of muscles, layers upon layers of them, arranged with the shortest ones nearest the bones and the longest ones nearest the skin. In the illustration below, we are looking at three vertebrae (shown in black) from the rear and at some of the short muscles (shown in rust)

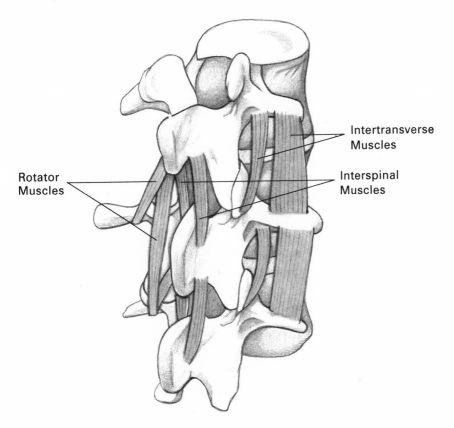

Intertransverse
Muscles

Interspinal
Muscles

Rotator
Muscles

THE MUSCLES OF THE SPINE

of the innermost layer. On the right, we see short muscles—the intertransverse muscles—that run vertically from each transverse process to the transverse process above. When these muscles are contracted, they pull the transverse processes closer together, using them as levers to help bend the spine to the right. Similarly, other short muscles—the interspinal muscles—run vertically from each spinous process to the next. When we tighten these, they draw the spinous processes together to bend the spine backward. In the drawing, we see still other short muscles—the rotator muscles—running diagonally, from the transverse process of one vertebra upward and inward to the spinous process of the vertebra above, and also from the transverse process of the bottom vertebra —skipping the middle vertebra—to the spinous process of the top one. When we contract these diagonal muscles, they twist or rotate the spine to the right. (The body has vertical and diagonal muscles on both sides of the vertebrae. Only one set is shown here for the sake of clarity.)

The illustration opposite (still showing the backbone from the rear) depicts some of the many layers of longer back muscles that lie over the short muscles shown on the previous page. On the right, we see medium-length muscles that begin at one vertebra and skip over as many as six other vertebrae before attaching themselves to another. On the left, we see some of the longest and largest back muscles, which cover the medium-length ones. These long, large back muscles are collectively called the *erector spinae*—Latin for erector of the spine. (In this illustration the erector spinae is shown as if cut off, to reveal the muscle layer beneath.)

The erector spinae runs the full length of the spine and is one of the most important movers and supporters of the spinal column. When the erector spinae is contracted, it arches the spine backward. If one side is tightened while the other is relaxed, it helps us bend sideways. It is the tension in the erector spinae and other back muscles that braces the spinal column from the rear, keeping it from falling forward—just as the tension in a sailboat's wire backstay (which runs from the top of the mast to the stern) keeps the mast from falling forward.

Covering the erector spinae are still more layers of muscles (not shown here) that in a sense are not true back muscles at all. That

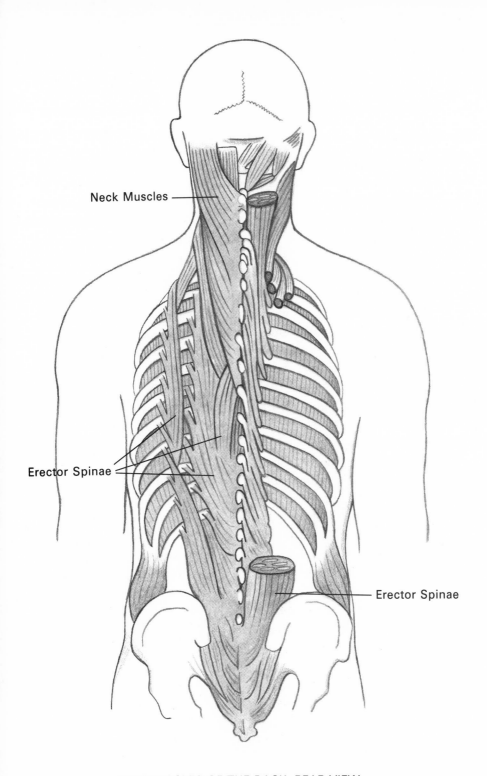

Neck Muscles

Erector Spinae

Erector Spinae

THE MUSCLES OF THE BACK, REAR VIEW

is, although they are attached to the vertebrae, their main job is not moving or supporting the spinal column; they merely use the spine as a solid purchase for moving some other part of the body. These "fake" back muscles include, in the chest region, muscles that primarily move the ribs and help us to breathe. In the upper back they are large muscles that mainly move the shoulders and arms. And in the lower back are other large muscles (including those forming the buttocks), which are attached to the hipbones, that primarily move the legs. In general, these ersatz back muscles are the ones whose contours we can see just below the skin. Thus, paradoxically, the familiar, visible muscles of the back are not true spinal muscles, while the real back muscles lie concealed deep beneath them.

When we look at the muscles of the front of the backbone, however, we see a very different situation than we did at the rear (see the illustration opposite). The neck has muscles all around it, but otherwise there are very few muscles attached to the front of the vertebrae—and the few that are there do not primarily move or support the spinal column. In the lower chest, the diaphragm (not shown in the illustration) is fastened to and partially covers some of the vertebrae, but its main job is to inflate the lungs. And in the lumbar region, a muscle called the *psoas* (also not shown) nestles on either side of the vertebrae, but its main job is to move the legs. Thus for much of the length of the spine, the front of the vertebrae lies virtually naked (except for ligaments) within the body.

With so few muscles on the front of the backbone, the job of bending the spinal column forward falls primarily to muscles not attached to the vertebrae at all. The aforementioned psoas muscle does help bend the spine to some degree, but most of the work of forward bending is done by the important muscles forming the abdominal wall (see the illustration). We have several layers of these abdominal muscles, which run in different directions. The inner layer runs diagonally from the hipbones upward and forward toward the ribs. Over these, another layer runs diagonally in the opposite direction from the hipbones upward and toward the rear, and the outer layer runs vertically. In the illustration, we see these outermost layers. When all of the layers of abdominal muscles are contracted, they bend the spine forward. If the muscles on one side are tightened while those on the other side are being relaxed, they pull the spine sideways.

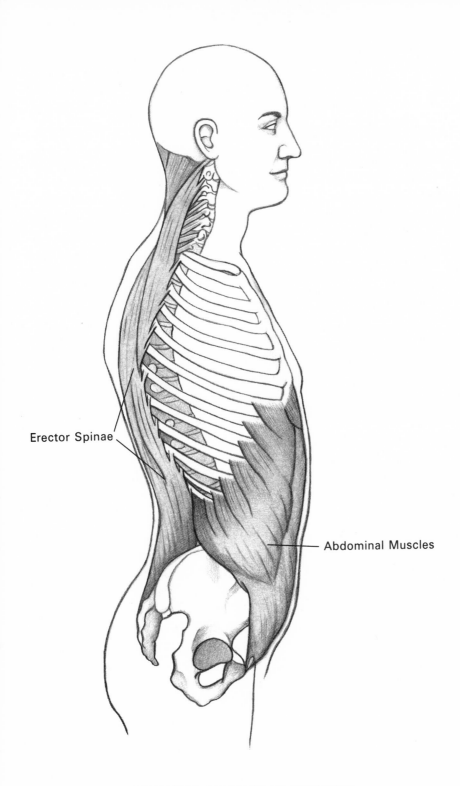

Erector Spinae

Abdominal Muscles

THE MUSCLES OF THE BACK, SIDE VIEW

In the chest region, the job of bracing the spinal column from the front is done largely by the ribs. Each of us has twelve pairs of ribs, attached at their rear to twelve thoracic (chest) vertebrae. The ribs then curve around the body like the hoops around a barrel, and most of them fasten to the breastbone in front, forming a fairly rigid bony cage. The rib cage markedly strengthens and stiffens this portion of the spine.

The lumbar region, however, does not have any such bony cage bracing it in front. Its sole support is provided by the several layers of abdominal muscles described above. The tension in these belly muscles keeps the spinal column from falling backward—just as the tension in a sailboat's wire forestay (which runs from the top of the mast to the bow) keeps the mast from toppling backward. This is the reason why it is so important for us all to keep the stomach muscles in good condition through exercise. Doing so will stabilize the spine and help prevent backaches. (Chapter 5 includes exercises that physicians most frequently recommend for strengthening these key abdominal muscles.)

How We Move

As the muscles of the torso contract, they are able to move the spinal column because it is segmented—that is, it is made up of many separate bones. If it had been designed, instead, as a single long bone —like a legbone, for example—we would naturally be unable to bend it. The individual vertebrae are able to move in relation to each other because the discs between them are so elastic that they can actually change their shape (see the illustration opposite). In the drawings, we are looking at two vertebrae from the front; we see the cylindrical bodies and the tips of the transverse processes on either side. In the top drawing, this section of the spine is bending toward the left. Notice that the disc itself has become more wedge-shaped, stretching and expanding on the outside of the bend, compressing and bulging on the inside of the bend. In the bottom drawing, the spinal section bends in the opposite direction, toward the right. Now the disc stretches at the left and becomes compressed and bulges to the right.

As we can see from the drawings, any single disc joint does not bend very far. The thick disc between the lowermost lumbar verte-

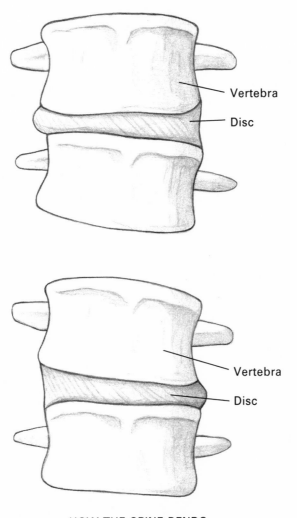

HOW THE SPINE BENDS

bra and the sacrum can bend the farthest, about 20 degrees backward and forward. But most of the other disc joints can bend only about ten degrees in any direction, and some of them no more than about five degrees. (The topmost neck joint, where the atlas swivels around the axis, is a special case. There is no disc between these two vertebrae; thus the joint can rotate about forty-five degrees.) These modest motions at the disc joints, however, when added together over the full length of the backbone, are enough to grant the human spine a remarkable range of overall motion.

All the many maneuvers one is able to perform with his or her back—from the graceful arabesque of a ballerina to the powerful swing of a baseball player—are made up of only four basic motions: bending forward, bending backward, bending sideways and rotating or twisting (see the illustrations below, opposite and on the following pages). The back bends most readily forward; most of us can flex the back far enough forward to touch the floor and look between the legs. Most of us can also arch the spine far enough backward to gaze straight up at the ceiling. We can bend the spine far enough sideways to reach nearly to the knee, and can twist it far

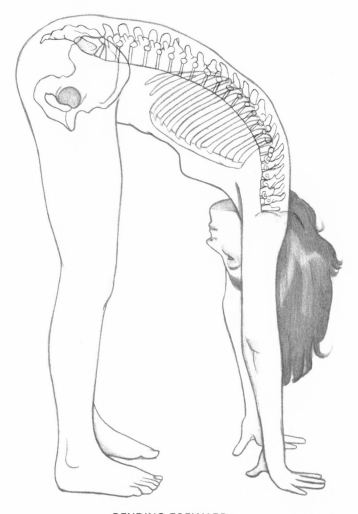

BENDING FORWARD

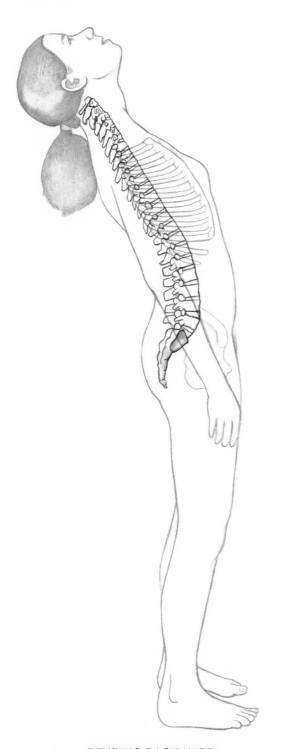

BENDING BACKWARD

enough around to see over the shoulder. Trained athletes sometimes can perform astonishing feats of spinal agility. Women Olympic gymnasts, for example, are able, from a prone position, to arch backward so far that they can touch their toes over their head to the balance beam. Most of us probably could not do this even with training. Such gymnasts usually are people who are unusually sup-

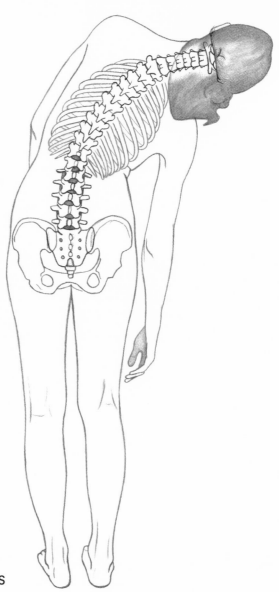

BENDING SIDEWAYS

ple to begin with. How far any one of us can bend or twist the spinal column in any direction is limited by many anatomical factors: for example, the locations and tightness of ligaments and muscles; the size and shape, as well as the elasticity, of discs; subtle variations in the shape of individual vertebrae; and the way some vertebrae are attached to other bones.

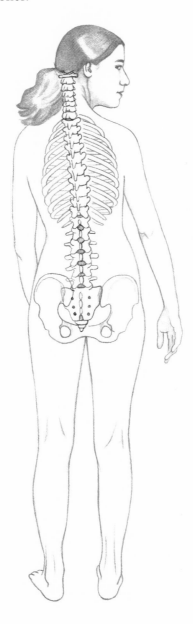

TWISTING

The four regions of the spine differ significantly in their flexibility. The neck is the most flexible part. It is amply endowed with muscles all around; its discs are relatively thick, and it can be moved easily in all directions. The chest region is fairly stiff. The discs are thinner here, but more importantly, the rib cage, which braces this part of the spine, also prevents it from bending very far. And in this region, too, the spinous processes overlap like shingles, further preventing much backward bending. The lumbar region is relatively flexible because the discs in this area are thick and it has no rib cage to stiffen it. The lumbar region can be bent freely forward and backward, but—unlike the neck—it cannot be twisted very far. This is partly due to the facet joints, which face in slightly different directions in different parts of the spine. Here in the lumbar region their interlocking surfaces are generally vertical and thus block rotation of the vertebrae.

The sacral region is the least flexible part of the spine. The sacrum is tightly wedged between the two hipbones, each of which consists of three bones (the *ilium, ischium* and *pubis*) fused into a solid mass. The sacrum is firmly attached to the two ilia, one on either side, by the *sacroiliac joints,* which are among the strongest and most stable joints in the body. Normally the sacroiliac joints can be moved only very slightly. Thus when we move the sacrum, we also move the hipbones, and when we move the hips, the sacrum moves too.

The backbone thus consists in effect of two flexible rods (the neck and lumbar regions) on either end of a stiff rod (the thoracic region) and mounted at its base on a solid pedestal (the sacrum). If we study the illustrations of the spine's four basic motions, we can readily see the regional differences in the spine's flexibility. When we bend forward, the thoracic regions bend some, but the neck and lumbar regions bend more (enough to straighten out their normal backward curvature). Notice that the spinous processes spread apart on the outside of the bend, and notice also that much of this forward flexibility is not in the spine at all but in the hip joints, which rock forward on the legs. (When people cannot touch their toes it is often because the muscles along the backs of their legs are tight.) When we arch backward, the stiffness of the chest is even more apparent. Most of the motion is in the neck and lumbar area, where the spinous processes squeeze closer together. When we bend sideways, the rib cage again limits how far the thoracic section can bend. While the ribs spread apart on the left, they come so close on the right, on the inside of the bend, that they almost touch. When we rotate the spine, the upper thoracic and the lumbar regions remain relatively straight partly because of the facet joints, while the twisting takes place in the lower thoracic region and to a greater extent in the neck. But when we perform this task during the course of our daily life—for example, when we reach around to pick up something slightly behind us—we also tend to twist the shoulders.

The flexibility of the spine can change with back disease. Back disease can cause backache, we know, and numbness or muscle weakness in a distant limb can also be a sign of back trouble. Yet another symptom of back disease can be the loss of flexibility of the spine—that is, a stiff back.

Many physicians contend that the high prevalence of back trouble in the human species is a result of upright posture—a debatable thesis, which we shall discuss in Chapter 6. It seems clear, however, that the unique construction of the spine does help determine *where*, at least, some types of back disease occur.

As mentioned earlier, the slope of the sacrum's upper surface is a factor in the development of a condition called spondylolisthesis. The regional differences in the spine's flexibility also seem to be a factor in the development of some other conditions. In particular, they help determine where the back breaks. Fractures in the spine generally occur in two specific spots: just below the chest area, where the ribs are attached to the spine, and to a lesser extent just above this chest area. These two fracture-prone places are precisely where the stiff thoracic region joins the more flexible lumbar and neck regions.

The upright posture itself also contributes to the location of back disease simply because it concentrates so much of the weight on the lower spine. A four-footed creature has its body weight distributed more evenly along its horizontal backbone, and its lumbar region must support only the region's own weight. The lumbar region in humans, however, must also support the weight of the chest (with its ribs), the shoulders and forelimbs, and the heavy head.

This load on the lower spine has actually been measured, in a continuing series of experiments since the early 1960s, by Swedish scientist Alf L. Nachemson, M.D. Dr. Nachemson has devised a miniature pressure-sensitive instrument built into the tip of a needle that he can insert, with the guidance of x-rays, directly into a person's lumbar disc. With this instrument, Dr. Nachemson and his colleagues have discovered that, for example, when we are standing in an ordinary manner, the load is more than half of the total body weight. A 120-pound person has a load of about 70 pounds on his or her lumbar discs; and a 200-pound person, a load of about 120 pounds. This load on the lumbar spine, Dr. Nachemson and his colleagues have further discovered, increases enormously during many ordinary activities that we all perform every day.

Presumably because of this load, the lumbar spine is also the part of the back most likely to ache, and several specific types of back disease—among them ruptured discs and degenerative arthritis—are most likely to occur there. There are "formidable mechanical demands" on this part of our spine, Augustus A. White III, M.D., professor of orthopedic surgery at Harvard Medical School, and Manohar M. Panjabi, Ph.D., associate professor of biomechanics in surgery at Yale University School of Medicine, point out in their book *Clinical Biomechanics of the Spine.* "It is not surprising that the lumbar spine may not always be capable of meeting" these demands, they say.

But does this mean that the human spine is a poorly designed, inherently weak structure? Many physicians argue that it is, citing as evidence the simple fact that the species does have so much back trouble. Yet among the experts there is no unanimity on this question. Certainly the back is designed so soundly that it almost never —unlike our heart—fails so completely as to cause death. How well the back is designed is more a philosophical than a scientific question, observes Dr. Nachemson. He believes that the spine is designed very well. "It has stood up for many millions of years," Dr. Nachemson notes, "and it has proven to be a rather strong and good structure. I don't believe I would redesign it."

2

THE CHANGING BACK, FROM CONCEPTION TO OLD AGE

The extraordinarily complex structure of the human back described in Chapter 1 is actually one that exists for only a relatively brief period in life, during young adulthood. The back, like the rest of the body, is constantly, inexorably changing, from the time of conception into old age, at times rapidly, at other times almost imperceptibly. Some of these changes contribute significantly to back trouble.

The back is the first of the structures of the body to begin developing. Only three weeks after conception, when the embryo is still only a microscopic, relatively amorphous mass of cells, some of these cells begin forming a tiny, slightly stiff, but also flexible rod called the notochord. (*Noto-* comes from the Greek word for back, while *-chord* simply means cord.) This rodlike notochord is the first and the simplest of three successive "backbones"—of increasing complexity and stiffness—that will support the body as it develops. This notochord is also part of our heritage from our animal ancestors, an echo of our evolutionary past. Similar rodlike notochords are found in the bodies of the simplest backboned creatures and also in the embryos of all our fellow vertebrates during the earliest stages of their development.

As the human embryo develops, a groove forms along the back of the notochord. This groove deepens; its sides curl up and over, and they meet and close, forming a tube. Called the neural tube, this is the precursor of both the spinal cord and the brain. Occasionally, in these early weeks, this neural tube fails to form properly. This early malformation may produce, in the resulting baby, a disastrous birth defect, the most common serious congenital defect of the spine: spina bifida with meningomyelocele (see page 92).

Together, the embryonic notochord and neural tube define the major axes of the body: the head end and tail end, the right and left sides, the front and the back. In the next step in the development of the spine, several dozen tiny beadlike chunks of tissue line up in pairs on either side of the notochord and neural tube. These are the precursors of the vertebrae and back muscles. The embryo, now four weeks old, is still just a fifth of an inch long and weighs only a few thousandths of an ounce. The head end of the neural tube has dilated into a rudimentary brain, and the embryo already has a simple, functioning heart. But it does not yet look much like a human. The body is comprised mostly of the back and is curled into the shape of a C. It has only bulges where the head and arms and legs will be. And the embryo unmistakably possesses a true tail, tucked up in front almost touching the head end.

During the second month of life, with incredible rapidity, the embryo begins to look more like a miniature person. It develops not only a head but also a face—with eyes, ears, nose and mouth—and arms and legs complete with tiny fingers and toes. Inside the body, a second "backbone," one made out of fast-growing cartilage (the substance that forms the nose and ears), starts to replace the first. This cartilage "backbone" is stiffer than the notochord, yet still fairly flexible. Cartilage-forming centers, four of them for each vertebra-to-be, appear among the paired beads of tissue in the back and begin expanding around the neural tube, starting to form the vertebral rings that will protect the developing spinal cord. This second cartilage "backbone" thus also introduces another feature of the adult spine: unlike the notochord, it is segmented—that is, made up of many separate pieces (vertebrae) joined together. This segmentation will give the back greater flexibility. During this month, the embryo also quickly acquires much of the rest of the skeleton: shoulder blades, ribs, hip "bones," arm and leg "bones"—a temporary interior scaffolding fashioned in miniature out of cartilage.

During this same month, however, work also begins on the third and permanent backbone. This one *is* made out of bone—a harder and more rigid substance than cartilage, providing better protection for the spinal cord and also better support for the muscles. Within the still incomplete vertebrae of the chest area, bone-forming centers appear and also begin expanding, replacing the cartilage around them. The bone grows far more slowly than the cartilage, however. It will be months before such bone-forming centers appear in most of the rest of the vertebrae and decades before—as we will see—this permanent backbone is finished. By the end of the second month, however, the brain and muscles have developed enough to allow the embryo to move some, and it has the beginnings of most of the internal organs. The tail is disappearing, and the body is straightening out from its earlier C shape. Though it is still only a little over an inch long and weighs but a few hundredths of an ounce, it is no longer considered an embryo. It is now a fetus.

During the next seven months, the fetus increases in size at a rate faster than at any other time in its life, growing more than fifteen times in length, on the average, and more than three thousand times in weight. During the third month, its sex—determined at conception—declares itself in external anatomy. In the back, the cartilaginous spinal column and the spinal cord have been the same length up to now, with the tip of the cord reaching to the coccyx. But the brain and spinal cord mature earlier than the skeleton, and their growth slows while the vertebrae then grow faster than the cord. As a result, the tip of the cord recedes up inside the column. The notochord is fast disappearing, while the cartilage "backbone" is developing rapidly. In this third month, the cartilage-forming centers in each typical vertebra coalesce to complete the protective rings —begun only the month before—around the spinal cord. By the seventh month, work on the third and final backbone has reached the point where bone-forming centers have appeared within the cartilage of most of the vertebrae. The fetus has now for a while been able to move enough to enable the mother to feel it kicking, and the heartbeat is strong enough to be heard with a stethoscope. During these last two months of fetal life, the skeleton, which has been growing rather slowly, now rapidly increases in mass.

By the time the baby is born, its skeleton weighs over a pound, comprising 15 to 20 percent of the total birth weight, and has 270 individual bones (far more than the adult number of 206). The spinal column has grown so much longer than the spinal cord that the tip of the cord, which earlier reached to the coccyx, now reaches only to the middle of the lumbar vertebrae. The notochord is almost gone, but remnants of it persist between the vertebrae, forming the soft, jellylike nucleus of each disc. The second cartilage "backbone," however, still forms much of the spinal column. The third, bone backbone is far from complete. A typical vertebra (which in an adult is a solid ring of bone around the spinal cord) consists of three separate bones: one in front of the spinal cord, for the vertebral body, and two at the rear of the cord, one on either side—all surrounded by cartilage. At the base of the spine, the sacrum (a single bone in an adult and the largest in the spine) consists of five separate bones, growing within the cartilage surrounding them. The vestigial tailbone has no bone at all but is still entirely made of cartilage.

Nor is the baby born with the four distinctive curves of an adult spine (shown in the illustration on page 22). At the end of the first month of embryonic life, as mentioned earlier, the back had only a single curve. Supported by the notochord, it was curled in a C shape. As the body developed, the back straightens out markedly. At birth, with so much of the spine still cartilage, it is fairly flexible. The thoracic and sacral regions retain their original fetal curvature. The cervical region has started, slightly, to reverse this fetal curl, but the lumbar region is essentially straight. The neck curve develops as we learn to hold the head up and sit up, during the first year of life. And the lumbar curve develops as we begin to stand up and toddle about, balancing the upper spine upon the sacrum, toward the end of the first year.

Although the rate of growth after birth is considerably slower than it was during the fetal months, the actual increase in size is of course dramatic: the cartilage-and-bone skeleton doubles in height, from roughly twenty to forty inches, in the first four years. During these childhood years, the bony pieces of the typical vertebrae expand, replacing the cartilage around them until they finally join, completing the protective bony rings around the spinal cord—a process begun in embryonic life. In each vertebra, first the bones at the rear grow together, and then these join with the one in front, to close the ring and form a single bone. During the third year, these vertebral rings start closing in the neck. During the fourth and fifth years, those in the thoracic region close, and during the sixth year, those in the lumbar region are complete.

As the body continues to grow, these vertebral rings enlarge not by simple expansion but, like all bones, by simultaneously adding new bone and destroying old. For a ring to get bigger, new bone must be added to the outside of the ring at the same time old bone is removed from the inside, thus hollowing out the hole. These processes of making new bone while at the same time destroying old and of constantly reworking the shapes of bones are ones that continue, at varying rates, not only during the growing years but throughout life, with some important consequences for the back.

The rate of bone growth, slowing since birth, plateaus during late childhood and then increases sharply again during what is called the adolescent growth spurt; this starts at about age eight to ten in girls, and two years later in boys. The individual shoots up in height and the body also changes rapidly, reaching puberty at about ages eleven to fourteen in girls, thirteen to sixteen in boys. The skeleton, however, is still not complete. It now has 350 individual bones, far more than at birth, and new ones are still appearing. Five new secondary bone-forming centers appear in each typical vertebra: three at the tips of three of the processes at the rear of the vertebra, and two on the vertebral body, one around the rim of the upper surface and another around the rim of the lower. By about age eighteen in girls and twenty in boys, most of us reach what is essentially our full skeletal height—on the average, three and a third times the length at birth.

Occasionally, as a child starts this adolescent growth spurt, his or her spine will begin to curve abnormally, either from side to side or backward and forward too much. Fortunately, at this age, with the spine still growing and the backbone still able to be molded, if a boy or girl wears a specially designed brace throughout these years, it will usually prevent the abnormal curvature from becoming worse.

Not until well into the third decade of a person's life does the skeleton reach maturity. Not until the mid-twenties or later does the permanent backbone finally finish replacing the cartilage "backbone." In each typical vertebra, the five secondary bone-forming centers, which appeared in the teens, finish their growth and fuse

with the main part of the vertebra. At the base of the spine, the five
bones that make up the sacrum fuse into a single bone, the largest
in the spine. And the spinal cord, which once reached to the tip of
the coccyx, now reaches only to the uppermost lumbar vertebrae.
Even after this, however, the skeleton continues to change. The
bones still grow some, and it is often not until the middle of a
person's life that fusions between bones bring the number in the
body down to 206. In the backbone, further fusions, late in life,
sometimes join the coccyx to the sacrum.

No sooner have the bones of the spinal column completed their
growth, however, than other parts of the back—the intervertebral
discs—begin to degenerate with age. At birth, the nuclei of the discs
were nearly 90 percent water. When we are in our twenties, the
discs gradually begin to dry out and show signs of wear. The annulus fibrosus, the layers of fibers holding the nucleus of the disc in
place, becomes torn and frayed. Such degeneration is normal and
usually does not cause trouble in most people. In some people,
however, part of the interior of the disc may herniate out through
the torn annulus, causing back pain and other trouble. Such herniated discs—popularly called slipped discs—are a significant cause
of back disease among young and middle-aged adults. Beyond middle age, however, as the discs continue to degenerate they become
more stable and less likely to herniate.

As the discs dry out with age, they also lose height, gradually
deflating over the decades. As they do so, the vertebrae also settle
down and become closer together. This is one of the several reasons
why individuals tend to shrink in height with age, a phenomenon
that we will discuss in more detail below. While these spaces between the vertebrae are narrowing, other changes are also taking
place in the bones. As noted earlier, the body is constantly subtly
reworking the bones, changing their shapes in response to the
stresses upon them. As a result, during a person's middle years, the
vertebrae tend to develop, both around the rims of their bodies and
also at the facet joints at their rear, projecting ridges of bone called
osteophytes (bone spurs). In a study in Göteborg, Sweden, x-rays
of 195 adult men and women showed that of those in their forties,
72 percent had osteophytes on their vertebrae and 24 percent had
narrowed disc spaces. Of those twenty years older, in their sixties,

nearly all—97 percent—had osteophytes on their vertebrae and 60 percent had narrowed disc spaces. These common changes in the spine physicians call degenerative joint disease or degenerative arthritis or sometimes spondylosis, among other names. These changes are a significant cause of backache and stiffness, particularly among older people. Curiously, though, there is often little correlation between the appearance of a person's spine in x-rays and his or her symptoms. Physicians often see people whose spinal x-rays reveal considerable degenerative arthritis yet who have little back trouble, and, conversely, other people whose x-rays show few degenerative changes yet who are quite disabled by backaches.

As we noted earlier, throughout one's life the body is constantly making new bone and destroying old. During the growing years, new bone is made faster than old is destroyed, for a net increase in bone mass. With age, however, the balance between the two processes shifts, and gradually, after the forties, old bone is destroyed more rapidly than new bone is made, for a net loss in bone mass. Thus over the decades, as individuals continue to age, the bones become softer and more porous, a condition called osteoporosis. Again, while this softening of the bones occurs in most people, it causes little back trouble in most of us. Nevertheless, osteoporosis is a significant cause of backache in older people, particularly women. The vertebrae may become so soft that they crush down to a fraction of their original height. This collapse of vertebrae is another of the several reasons why men and women tend to shrink in height as they become older.

With age, the ligaments and muscles holding up the spinal column also become lax, and they allow the back to sag. The curves of the spine increase, particularly in the thoracic region, and we tend to hunch over. Because of this, as well as the flattening of the discs and the collapse of the vertebrae, we may lose several inches or more in height by the time we are elderly. This is such a common phenomenon that it was familiar more than two thousand years ago to the fifth century B.C. Greek physician Hippocrates, who in his writings on spinal curvatures observed that "the spine is liable to be bent from old age."

These degenerative changes in the back are as much a part of aging as wrinkles in the skin, gray hairs and blurring vision are.

Nevertheless, there is enormous variation among men and women in the extent of these changes. Just as some older people retain thick, dark hair or can see without glasses, not everyone develops back trouble. Backache is common as we become older, but it is not inevitable in every individual.

3

WHAT CAN GO WRONG

If you have a persistently aching back, there are many specific back diseases—ranging from the relatively benign to the extremely serious—that might be causing the trouble. However, many diseases that are not primarily back diseases may nonetheless first reveal themselves in the form of a backache. Mrs. Mary Draper, for instance, thought she had a back problem. Whenever she walked the one block from her office to the bank, she felt a pain in her lower back and legs so intense that she had to stop and rest several times on the way. She would window-shop to avoid notice. Yet it turned out that she did not have back trouble at all, but a blood vessel problem. Arteriosclerosis had totally blocked the two big arteries carrying blood to her legs, and she needed vascular—not back—surgery.

Other non-back diseases that can first show up as back pain include aortic aneurysms (ballooning of the main artery from the heart); stomach or duodenal ulcers; inflammation or cancer of the pancreas (a digestive gland near the stomach); many different kinds of kidney disease; lung cancer; cancer and other diseases of the prostate gland in men; breast cancer and cancer and other diseases of the ovaries and uterus in women.

Conversely, not all back diseases cause backaches. Mrs. Jane

Davis, a perky, dark-haired woman in her mid-fifties, had a condition called spinal stenosis severely enough to require back surgery. She was off work for more than six months, yet she never had back pain. "The pain would always start in my hips," she recalls, "and then go on down into my legs." Back disease also can be heralded by symptoms other than pain: stiffness or excessive flexibility of the spine; numbness, tingling, muscular weakness or even paralysis of the arms or the legs.

The back diseases that we will discuss in this chapter are diseases that have afflicted our species since before the dawn of history. Yet it was not until well into the twentieth century that physicians were able to do much about most of them. They could not even diagnose most of them before x-ray equipment became available. (Wilhelm Conrad Roentgen discovered x-rays in 1895 and won the Nobel Prize for the discovery in 1901.) Modern medicine has since virtually wiped out some back diseases and vastly improved the treatment of others. (Before the advent of antibiotic drugs, for instance, many people were crippled by tuberculosis of the spine.) Today, physicians can effectively treat some diseases and deformities that only a generation ago people had no choice but to live with.

Ironically, twentieth-century medicine has also at the same time enormously increased the prevalence of certain back diseases. Because so many more people are living longer—the life expectancy in this country has increased from less than fifty years for a baby born in 1900 to more than seventy years for one born today—there are many more people around afflicted with degenerative arthritis and osteoporosis, both diseases associated with aging. If there is a modern "epidemic" of backache in the United States, as so many popular magazine articles imply, it is largely due to this increase in our longevity. In the countries of Western Europe and other developed areas, the mix of back diseases is the same as it is in the United States: little back disease due to tuberculosis and much back disease due to the degenerative changes of aging. In the less developed countries, however, where there is poorer sanitation, nutrition and medical care, the pattern of back disease is the same as it was in this country a century ago: more tuberculosis of the spine and less disease due to aging, because people do not live as long.

Many of the non-back diseases that can cause back pain are serious, and some of the back diseases can be. Because of the intimate anatomical relationship between our vertebrae and our spinal cord and nerve roots, back disease can sometimes threaten the functioning of nerves and can cause muscular weakness or—if not treated promptly—permanent paralysis or even death, as we will see in this chapter. This is why, if you have persistent back pain, you should consult a physician to find out what is causing it. In Chapter 4 we will discuss the specific symptoms, or danger signs, that should impel you to see a physician about your back.

The following are the major diseases that afflict the human spine.

Herniated Disc

One common sign of back trouble is the excruciating pain called *sciatica* because it follows the course of the sciatic nerve, the largest nerve in the body. The sciatic nerves are formed in the hip region, one on each side, by the combination of several nerves that emerge from the lower part of the spine. In the illustration on page 54 the course of the sciatic nerve and its branches are depicted in rust. From the hip region, it runs down the back of each thigh as far as the knee, where it branches into other nerves. Sciatic pain, following this nerve pathway, begins in the low back and radiates into the hip and buttock and on down the back of the thigh, sometimes as far as the calf and foot.

This distinctive pattern of pain has been recognized for thousands of years. In the fifth century B.C., the Greek physician Hippocrates noted that the Scythians were particularly afflicted with it, because, he thought, they spent so much time on horseback. Five hundred years later, the Roman Pliny the Elder offered a couple of remedies for it: an herb he called hiberis and a concoction made from earthworm washings. And in seventeenth-century England, Shakespeare knew of sciatica's agony; he included it in a string of curses uttered by Timon of Athens: "Thou cold sciatica,/Cripple our senators."

Yet it was not until well into the twentieth century that physicians figured out what causes this ancient pain. In the 1930s, two physicians, Joseph S. Barr, M.D., and Jason Mixter, M.D., at Boston's Massachusetts General Hospital discovered that sciatica could be caused by the herniation of an intervertebral disc. It is now

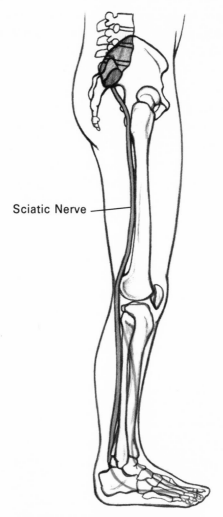

Sciatic Nerve —

THE PATHWAY OF SCIATICA

known that *herniated disc* is the major cause of sciatica, and that sciatica also can be caused by a number of other conditions, including infections, injuries, tumors, degenerative arthritis and spondylolisthesis (see page 86)—anything that presses on or stretches a root of the sciatic nerve.

A herniated disc is the condition popularly called a slipped disc, which is a misnomer. The intervertebral discs are tightly bonded between the bodies of the vertebrae and cannot slip out of place. What they can do is shown in the illustration opposite. As we age, the discs degenerate and dry out, and the annular fibers holding the disc nucleus in place become torn. Since a disc has a high internal pressure, it can blow out through these torn fibers, forming a blister-like bulge. In the drawing, such a herniation is shown in rust at the rear of one disc. For comparison, a normal disc is shown below the diseased one. Such a bulging disc may compress nerves in the spine, and the symptoms it causes depend upon which nerve or nerves it compresses. If a herniated disc presses upon any of the several roots of the sciatic nerve, the person affected will feel the distinctive pain of sciatica and also may have numbness or muscular weakness in the affected leg. If the ruptured disc presses instead on nerve roots in the neck, the person may feel pain shooting down an arm and have numbness and muscle weakness in the hand and fingers. Or if the disc presses nerves in the cauda equina, the continuation of the spinal cord supplying the bladder and bowels, the person may have trouble urinating or defecating.

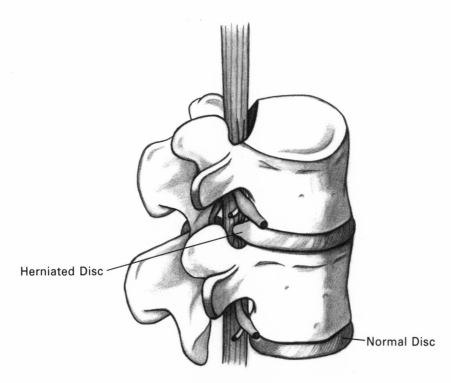

Herniated Disc

Normal Disc

A HERNIATED DISC

The many intervertebral discs are not all equally likely to herniate. The ones that most frequently do are concentrated in two specific locations in the spine. In the illustration opposite, these two herniation-prone places are shown in rust: the two lowermost discs in the lumbar region and, to a lesser extent, the two lowermost discs in the neck. These are the two locations that are subject to the greatest stress because they are mobile areas of the spine adjacent to stiff sections: the flexible lower lumbar region next to the stiff sacrum, and the lower neck region next to the stiff thoracic section. And the lower lumbar discs, which herniate the most often, are also the ones that bear most of the body's weight.

Among humans, herniated discs are a common cause of back trouble. According to the National Center for Health Statistics' (NCHS) Health Interview Survey, there are more than two and a half million men and women in the United States with displaced discs, half of them with trouble severe enough that they saw a doctor or had to limit their activities. Statistics also show that herniated disc is a disease of young and middle-aged adults. According to epidemiological studies, the incidence of herniated disc is highest among people in their twenties, thirties and forties, and the number of cases drops sharply in people over sixty. Beyond middle age, as the discs continue to degenerate and dry out, they seem to become more stable and less likely to herniate.

A study conducted during the 1970s by Jennifer L. Kelsey, Ph.D., of the Yale University School of Medicine has identified some other factors influencing why some peoples' discs herniate and others do not. In an analysis of over two hundred people with herniated lumbar discs matched to people without, Dr. Kelsey found that those with sedentary jobs and those who spend half or more of their job time driving a motor vehicle are more likely to rupture discs. Truck drivers in particular, she found, are almost five times more likely to herniate a disc than other people. Other researchers have suggested that the amount of heavy lifting many truck drivers do may be a significant factor in their herniating discs, but in Dr. Kelsey's study heavy manual work did not appear to be an important factor.

When a person's disc blows, so to speak, sometimes it goes suddenly and dramatically when a person exerts only a modest effort.

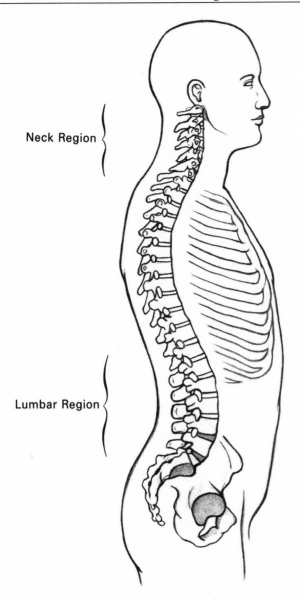

Neck Region

Lumbar Region

DISCS MOST LIKELY TO HERNIATE

People have ruptured discs reaching for tennis balls, lifting groceries out of a car or slipping off boats. When a disc herniates suddenly with such a slight exertion, it is because the actual rupture is only the final stage in a long process of degeneration that has been going on for some time. Other times, however, a disc may bulge so gradually over a period of time that it causes recurring trouble on and off for years.

Paula Harris, a tall, clear-eyed woman with short reddish-brown hair, is a hard-working mother with four young children, two boys and two girls ranging from nine months to nine years, and a husband who travels frequently. Mrs. Harris, now thirty, has been fighting back trouble for nearly ten years. Several times a year she would have what she calls "one of my usual three-day spells" of sciatica. She describes the pain as being similar to someone "twisting a knife in your hipbone, yet the whole leg is numb all the way to the toes. And the nerve just keeps pounding. Boom! Boom! Boom!" Recently Mrs. Harris had her "worst spell yet," and her doctor had her undergo *myelography*, a special type of x-ray, to pinpoint her problem. The myelogram showed that she has a slight bulge on the rear of one disc, the one just above the lowest lumbar vertebra.

Paula Harris' symptoms are not now severe enough to necessitate surgery. Her doctor is therefore treating her with conservative care, a phrase physicians use for nonsurgical treatments—pain-relieving drugs, traction, braces, massage, heat—also appropriate for many different types of back disease. Conservative care works for most people with herniated discs, and particularly for those whose diseased discs are in the neck. For these people, physicians often recommend that they wear an orthopedic collar for a while to relieve the afflicted disc by immobilizing the neck. For Paula Harris, whose bulging disc was in her lumbar region, her physician prescribed complete bed rest at home—one of the most common treatments for back disease. This would reduce the pressure on her disc and give it time to heal itself.

For a busy young mother, complete bed rest at home is not easy. With four small children, Paula Harris had to round up her husband, her mother, her sisters, and even her seventy-five-year-old mother-in-law to help out. For the first few weeks she could not get up at all, and then she was able to begin getting up half an hour each day. After four or five weeks, however, she became quite depressed when "it just didn't seem to be getting any better." But then gradually it finally did start getting better.

In order for Paula Harris to avoid disc surgery, however, her doctor has also recommended that she take a number of other measures to reduce the pressure on her low back—things that only she herself can do. "I never was sensible about my back until this last attack," she admits. "Then I began to realize that I did have to take better care of myself. I'm now trying to rearrange my lifestyle around my back." Specifically, her doctor suggested that she lose weight and cut down on the amount of heavy lifting she does. She is also to strengthen her abdominal muscles by exercise so that they will support her spine better. The measures Mrs. Harris is taking to stave off surgery—things any of us can do to help our back—are discussed at greater length in Chapter 5.

If a ruptured disc, however, presses upon a nerve root in such a way as to cause a muscular weakness or interfere with bowel or bladder function, most physicians recommend immediate surgery to remove the disc and thus relieve the pressure on the nerve. Such surgery is called a *diskectomy* (literally, removal of a disc) or sometimes a laminectomy, because surgeons usually cut through the lamina of a vertebra (the portion between the spinous and transverse processes) to get at the disc. Only part of the disc is removed—the displaced portion and as much of the soft interior as can be scooped out, leaving most of the fibrous annulus in place. Such disc surgery is probably the most common of all back operations. According to the National Center for Health Statistics' National Hospital Discharge Survey, 149,000 men and women in the United States underwent diskectomies in one recent year.

The muscular weakness that necessitates such surgery can be extremely subtle, so subtle that the person may not even be aware of it. Bob Alvarez, a handsome bachelor in his early thirties who sells advertising for a television station, had back trouble on and off for several years. Then one evening "a young lady was giving me a back rub," he laughs, "and all of a sudden, my back just kind of went *bwong!* I never felt pain that badly." In one diagnostic test, his doctor had Mr. Alvarez pull up with his foot against the doctor's hand, a task Mr. Alvarez could not perform with his left foot. "I was shocked," he recalls. "My foot didn't have any strength at all." The muscle down the front of his lower leg was completely out, his doctor explained, resulting in a condition doctors call foot drop.

When Mr. Alvarez walked, his left foot flopped on the floor. A myelogram confirmed that he had a sizable protrusion on one of his lumbar discs.

Without surgery, Mr. Alvarez faced the possibility of permanent paralysis of some muscles in his left leg—a risk that had to be balanced against the risk of the surgery itself. Mr. Alvarez's physician told him that with surgery, he had about a 90 percent chance of recovering full use of his leg. Mr. Alvarez felt that he had little choice.

When Mr. Alvarez woke up in the recovery room after surgery, he was surprised to discover that "the pain was essentially gone. I had been afraid of the pain that would occur after the operation just from the incision. Compared to the pain I had had before the surgery, it was such a relief that I hardly felt the incision." He spent twelve days in the hospital, seven of them after surgery, and his doctor allowed him—since he does not work with his back—to return to work three and a half weeks after the operation. If Mr. Alvarez had had a job that did involve working with his back, his physician would not have allowed him to return for perhaps three months. Mr. Alvarez is, however, "taking things slowly, because I don't want to go through any of that again." Two and a half months after surgery, he is walking (but not jogging) to keep in condition, avoiding lifting, and doing gentle exercises to strengthen the muscles supporting his spine.

In the 1960s a new treatment was introduced that seemed for a while to offer an alternative to surgery for people like Mr. Alvarez. An enzyme called chymopapain, it is derived from papaya fruit and is related to the active substance in meat tenderizer. When chymopapain is injected into a diseased disc, it can dissolve some of the disc substance. The drug, however, has become entangled in controversy. In the mid-1970s a still-disputed study failed to prove that chymopapain injections are any more effective than injections of a placebo, and the Food and Drug Administration did not approve the drug for general use in the United States. (It remains in use in some other countries.) A new study of chymopapain's effectiveness is underway in this country that may resolve the controversy.

Degenerative Arthritis

The word "arthritis" simply means an inflammation of a joint. Yet according to the National Institute of Arthritis, Diabetes, and Digestive and Kidney Diseases, there are one hundred or more different types of arthritis ranging in their impact upon a person's life from extremely serious to almost trivial. Three major forms of arthritis affect the spine: degenerative arthritis, rheumatoid arthritis and ankylosing spondylitis. Of these three, *degenerative arthritis* is overwhelmingly the most common and the least serious.

Physicians use a bewildering variety of names for this widespread phenomenon—among them, *osteoarthritis, osteoarthrosis, wear-and-tear arthritis, old-age arthritis, degenerative joint disease, degenerative disc disease* and sometimes *spondylosis.* The word "arthritis" is actually not a strictly accurate one for this condition, since this degenerative process is *not* primarily an inflammation. However, we will continue—with apologies to the etymological purists—to call it degenerative arthritis because so many people do.

Degenerative arthritis has one of the longest lineages of any disease; signs of it have been found on the bones of dinosaurs, prehistoric cavemen and ancient Egyptian mummies. It is also one of the most widespread of diseases, affecting many of our fellow vertebrates: birds, mice (but, curiously, not rats), rabbits, dogs, horses, some breeds of cattle and swine, and baboons. Today, degenerative arthritis affects some 16 million Americans. It is a disease we will probably all develop if we live long enough.

Degenerative arthritis seems to be part of the normal biological process of aging. As we grow older, the joints eventually tend to wear out. The cartilage lining and protecting the joint surfaces wears away, and the underlying bone often changes shape. The joints most affected are those in the areas that bear the most weight or otherwise get the most use: our hands, feet, knees, hips—and the spine. Degenerative arthritis is largely a local phenomenon, not a body-wide illness.

In the spine, degenerative arthritis most often develops in the places most subject to stress, the very same places where discs tend to herniate: the lower part of the neck and the lower part of our lumbar region. What happens in the spine is depicted in the illustration below, which shows the three lowermost lumbar vertebrae, the sacrum and coccyx. As the intervertebral discs dry out with age, they lose their pressure and deflate, thus occupying less space. In the illustration, the two lowermost discs have become so flat that their disc spaces are narrowed, while the uppermost disc is still normal. As a result of such disc space narrowing, the vertebrae inevitably settle down and become closer together. This altered geometry at the disc joint changes the stresses upon the vertebrae, and they— which, like all bones, are constantly changing shape in response to demands made upon them—respond by developing pronounced ridges of bone around their upper and lower rims. These ridges are called *osteophytes* (*osteo-* means bone, and *-phyte* is a pathological growth) or, popularly, spurs. In the drawing, such osteophytes are

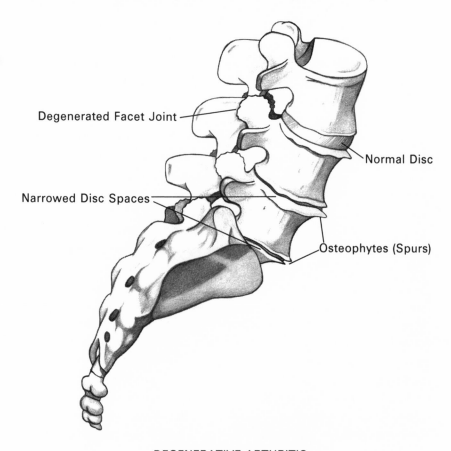

DEGENERATIVE ARTHRITIS

shown around the upper and lower rims of the two lowermost lumbar vertebrae. The settling of the vertebrae also causes the facet joints at the rear to become misaligned. Their cartilage, too, may thin out, and they may also develop osteophytes. Rarely, a pair of vertebrae may actually become fused.

Studies in Leigh, England, have demonstrated how common such changes in the spine are. X-rays of people between the ages of fifty-five and sixty-four showed that 41 percent of the men and 27 percent of the women had narrowed disc spaces and osteophytes in the neck, and 23 percent of the men and 13 percent of the women had them in the lumbar area.

Other studies in this country have underscored the relationship between degenerative arthritis and aging. In a National Center for Health Statistics' Health Examination Survey, x-rays of hands and feet showed that 30 percent of men and 20 percent of women between the ages of thirty-five and forty-four had degenerative arthritis. Among people fifty-five to sixty-four, 63 percent of the men and 75 percent of the women had it, and by the time people reached the ages of seventy-five to seventy-nine, 81 percent of the men and 90 percent of the women had developed it.

Yet there is more to the development of degenerative arthritis than just aging. Another factor seems to be cumulative mechanical stress over a lifetime. The Leigh, England, study cited above also found that the men who mined coal had significantly more degenerative arthritis, particularly in the lumbar region, than other men: 79 percent of the miners were affected. And there must also be hereditary factors that help determine why some people develop degenerative arthritis earlier or more severely than others.

It is easy to understand how narrowed disc spaces and misaligned facet joints might cause muscle strains and backaches (although most physicians agree that the narrowing of a single disc space is unlikely to cause significant pain). Like herniated discs, osteophytes can press against nerves and cause numbness or muscular weakness. But most people with such degenerative changes in their spines have little trouble with them. There is no correlation between what a spine looks like in x-rays and how it feels. One person may have several narrowed disc spaces and long osteophytes and no back pain while another may have only slight degenerative changes visible in x-rays and yet be completely disabled. Also, such degenerative changes, once they occur, are permanent, but backaches come and go.

Such degenerative changes *are,* however, a common cause of both neck and back pain. An older person whose neck or back aches a bit occasionally or who is somewhat stiff and creaky when he or she first gets out of bed in the morning probably has degenerative arthritis. And most such people can keep periodic aches and pains under control by resting the back judiciously when it hurts, taking a mild pain reliever from time to time, and—when the back does not hurt—exercising to strengthen the abdominal muscles.

People who do develop degenerative arthritis at a younger age or more severely than average may find they must reorganize their lives around the disease. Mr. Oliver Ballard, for instance, is a young-looking sixty-three-year-old, slender and trim, with thick steely-gray hair, but he has the back, his doctor tells him, of an eighty-year-old man, with osteophytes on almost every vertebra. Mr. Ballard's bad back has been "a nagging thing" all his life. About eight years ago, when he was in his mid-fifties, the situation became critical enough to force him to retire early from his business, a piano store. "It's heavy work," he explains. "If you're in the piano business, you move pianos even when you own the store."

Oliver Ballard has worn orthopedic corsets intermittently for years to help support his spine, and now finds he must wear one "pretty much all the time. When I get up in the morning, by the time I walk over to where the corset is, my back hurts enough that I know I'd better put it on. And"—he chuckles ruefully—"it's only about fifteen feet away!" Mr. Ballard now never tests his back, he explains, "because I know there is nothing there." On a recent trip to Turkey, Greece and Russia, "my poor wife was carrying all the luggage—and, almost, me." And to pursue his favorite pastime of camping outdoors, he has sought out a backpack that lets him carry all the weight on his hips.

Surgery can sometimes help people with degenerative arthritis. If an osteophyte is pressing on a nerve, a surgeon can relieve the pressure, or if a spine has become unstable, fusing vertebrae may stabilize it. But in Mr. Ballard's case, surgery cannot help him; the disease affects too many of his vertebrae.

Mr. Ballard is a back cripple; he no longer has full use of his back. Yet like so many people with serious back trouble, you would never know it to look at him. He looks perfectly normal. And while his bad back dominates his life, he would rather talk about anything else —his love of hiking, his favorite national parks. "The back is something you just live with."

Rheumatoid Arthritis

In contrast to degenerative arthritis, *rheumatoid arthritis* is a much less common but also much more serious disease. While rheumatoid arthritis is not primarily a back disease, when it does attack the spinal column, it is one of the few back problems that can be life-threatening.

Rheumatoid arthritis is a true arthritis, an inflammation of the joints. Unlike degenerative arthritis, it is also a body-wide illness; people with rheumatoid arthritis often feel generally tired and sick and may run a fever. The disease begins as an inflammation in tissues called the synovial membranes, which form portions of many of the joints, including the small facet joints at the rear of the spinal column. The disease causes an affected joint to swell and become stiff and painful, and in time it can eat away and destroy not only the joint but also other nearby tissues. Rheumatoid arthritis most frequently attacks the joints of the hands, wrists, elbows, feet, knees, hips, and not uncommonly, the spine. One of the most painful and crippling of chronic diseases, it affects some 6.5 million Americans. For reasons no one yet knows, it strikes women three times as often as men.

Today the cause of this disease still remains unknown. In the 1970s, researchers discovered a strong clue that there is a genetic factor: 59 percent of people with rheumatoid arthritis have a protein molecule dubbed DW4 on their cell surfaces, while less than 20 percent of people without the disease have this protein. Scientists now suspect that rheumatoid arthritis is triggered by some as-yet-unidentified virus, and that an inherited malfunctioning of the person's immune system is also somehow involved.

Rheumatoid arthritis most often begins when people are between the ages of twenty and sixty. In order to diagnose rheumatoid arthritis, physicians must use a number of diagnostic procedures, including testing the blood for an antibody called rheumatoid factor that is present in the serum of most (but not all) people with the disease.

Rheumatoid arthritis is a very unpredictable disease. While there is no cure and the damage to joints is largely irreversible, in most people the disease can be kept under control by a careful combination of treatments, often supervised by medical specialists called rheumatologists. Drugs can relieve pain and reduce the inflammation. The most widely used drug is aspirin in large doses; and if this does not work or has too many side effects, physicians may prescribe any one of many other drugs, including cortisone, gold salts and other anti-inflammatory drugs. People with rheumatoid arthritis usually must also regularly perform certain exercises specifically prescribed for the affected joints, to keep them from stiffening and to prevent as much deformity as possible. In severe cases, people may need to wear a brace or splint or may require surgery.

While rheumatoid arthritis does not usually begin in the spine, it frequently spreads there. When it does, it usually attacks the neck vertebrae in the manner depicted in the illustration opposite, which shows all seven neck vertebrae. In the drawing, the disease has damaged the small facet joints in the upper part of the neck, although the lowermost facet joint of the neck remains normal. The disease has also destroyed several of the intervertebral discs and eaten away parts of the adjacent vertebrae; the disc spaces are thinner, and the vertebrae have settled down upon each other. (In rheumatoid arthritis, however, the vertebrae do not develop the projecting osteophytes so characteristic of degenerative arthritis.) The most serious consequence of rheumatoid arthritis in the spine comes when the disease destroys the topmost joint of the spine, the one between the atlas and the axis. If this happens, the atlas can become displaced, sliding forward on the second vertebra as shown in the drawing. This can have catastrophic consequences, as we shall see.

Mrs. Joan Marchi, a cheerful suburban matron in her mid-fifties, has had severe rheumatoid arthritis for eight years. Her hands are so crippled that she has needed several operations on them, and her feet and knees are so weakened that she must sometimes use a cane. Early last year she began having pain in the middle of her back and

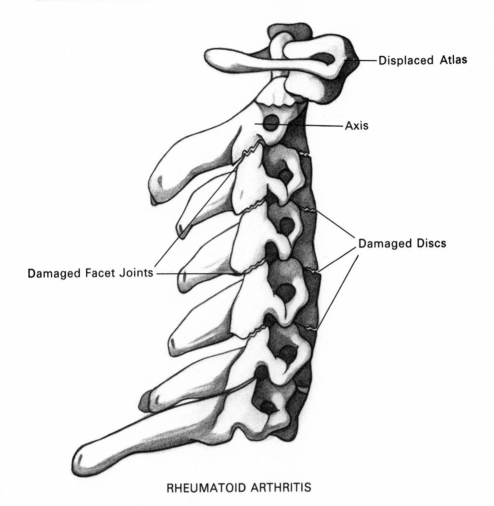

Displaced Atlas

Axis

Damaged Discs

Damaged Facet Joints

RHEUMATOID ARTHRITIS

her neck, but it never occurred to her that this might have anything to do with her arthritis. She was having a particularly busy year: she was serving as president of the PTA, was supervising a major redecoration of her home and was touring prospective colleges with her son, a high school junior.

Then her back got worse. "If I moved too quickly or if I turned in bed, I would get these pains as though someone had taken a hot poker and thrust it right up the back of my head. It was the most frightening thing that I have ever experienced." When she went to a doctor, x-rays of her neck showed that she was literally on the brink of death. The arthritis had invaded her spine and had badly weakened the ligaments that normally hold the atlas in place on top of the axis. Her atlas, along with her entire skull, was sliding forward on the second vertebra. At any moment her atlas might slip further and sever her spinal cord, instantly turning her into a quadriplegic or killing her. Mrs. Marchi had no choice but prompt surgery, and in the few days before it could be scheduled, she had to be very, very careful. "Do not sneeze," she recalls the surgeon telling her. "If you sneeze or fall down or bump something, you may not make it to the operating table."

The surgeon stabilized the joint by fusing the vertebrae to her skull, and although Mrs. Marchi had to spend eleven weeks in traction afterwards (several weeks in the hospital and the rest at home) and another seven weeks wearing a soft orthopedic collar, she is forever grateful to her surgeon. "He truly saved my life."

Ankylosing Spondylitis

Robert Van Dyck is an urbane and witty man in his late forties, with friendly brown eyes and a boyish thatch of brown hair. He stands and walks, however, as he puts it, "half like an ape," with his spine perpetually stiff and hunched over and his head tilted forward so he faces the ground. To look a visitor in the eye, he must roll his eyes upward and peer over the top of his glasses. He eases himself into a chair, bending only at the hips, and demonstrates that he can turn his head from side to side no more than half an inch.

Mr. Van Dyck is the victim of the third form of arthritis that can affect the spine: *ankylosing spondylitis*, a disease also often called *stiff spine, frozen spine, poker spine, ankylosing spondyloarthrosis* and *Marie-Strümpell disease* (after two nineteenth-century physicians who studied it). It is far less common than either degenerative or rheumatoid arthritis, affecting about two out of every thousand people. In contrast to rheumatoid arthritis, it strikes men more than twice as often as women.

Ankylosing spondylitis typically begins when a person is in his or her twenties (Robert Van Dyck was in college when he learned he had the disease) as pain and stiffness in the lower back that may persist over a period of months or years. The inflammatory process usually starts in the base of the spine and the sacroiliac joints and over a period of years slowly, insidiously moves up the spinal column. It attacks the intervertebral discs in particular, destroying the fibrocartilage and replacing it with scar tissue that gradually ossifies (turns to bone), thus fusing the vertebrae together into a solid, rigid rod. In the illustration below, the enlarged "window" into the man's spine shows six vertebrae that thus have been fused by ossified discs into a single, stiff structure. (The word "ankylosing" means fusing, and "spondylitis" means inflammation of the vertebrae.)

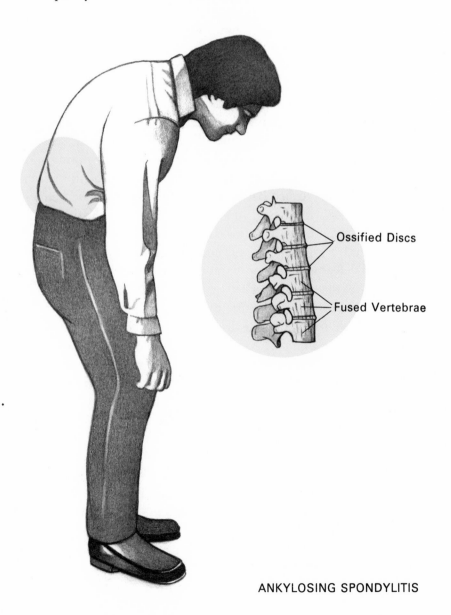

Ossified Discs

Fused Vertebrae

ANKYLOSING SPONDYLITIS

The final outcome of the disease is quite variable and unpredictable. While Mr. Van Dyck's spine is totally fused from top to bottom, sometimes the disease will fuse just a few of the lower lumbar vertebrae, leaving the person aware only of some stiffness. Other times it will hunch a person over until he or she is almost unable to see ahead, as shown in the illustration on the previous page. And the disease may also attack the hips and shoulders, further crippling the person.

Ankylosing spondylitis dates back at least to ancient Egypt. Ramses II, who ruled from 1292 to 1225 B.C., had a spine so stiff and curved that his head was bent forward and he could take only tiny steps—but he lived to about the age of ninety. Yet today what causes ankylosing spondylitis remains as much a mystery as what causes rheumatoid arthritis. Researchers are, however, pursuing very similar clues for these two dissimilar diseases. In the 1970s, scientists discovered that about 90 percent of people with ankylosing spondylitis have on their cell surfaces a characteristic protein molecule —but a molecule (called B27) different from the one associated with rheumatoid arthritis. Less than 10 percent of people who do not have ankylosing spondylitis have this B27 molecule. This finding strongly points toward a genetic factor, and researchers suspect that some inherited defect in a person's immune system may be involved. The discovery of this association between ankylosing spondylitis and B27 protein has prompted scientists to look harder at people with B27, and they have found that the disease seems to be far more common than previously thought. A number of people seem to have it in a form so mild and insignificant that they are not aware of it.

Physicians diagnose ankylosing spondylitis partly on the basis of its appearance on x-rays. The disease leaves the ossified discs bulging slightly. Doctors call this bamboo spine because these bulges resemble the nodes in a stalk of bamboo. However, early in the disease x-rays may be negative. Doctors also test the blood; a person with ankylosing spondylitis is likely to have the B27 protein but will *not* have rheumatoid factor, the antibody associated with rheumatoid arthritis. Another simple but important test is measuring a person's chest expansion—that is, the difference between the diameter of the chest when it is full of air and when all the air is blown out. Ankylosing spondylitis can also fuse the ends of a person's ribs so that he is unable to move them normally and must breathe with his stomach muscles. If a person's chest expansion is less than two inches, physicians are likely to suspect ankylosing spondylitis.

If a person does have ankylosing spondylitis, it is important to diagnose it as soon as possible so that proper treatment can begin. Physicians can prescribe a number of different pain-relieving and anti-inflammatory drugs. They may also recommend that to minimize any eventual deformity, a person with ankylosing spondylitis watch his posture, holding himself as erect as possible during the day and sleeping with his spine straight at night. These positions, however, are not always the most comfortable ones for a person with this disease. Doctors may prescribe deep breathing exercises and special exercises designed to keep the spine and other joints as flexible as possible.

With such treatment, most people with ankylosing spondylitis can lead normal lives. Yet the disease can have an enormous impact, as it has on Robert Van Dyck. He has had a great deal of pain, which is not inevitable with the disease. "The pain roved my body. I'd have it in the legs, the back, the hip area. Excruciating spasms occurred in the neck." This pain has kept him from marrying. "I have enough problems with myself," he says, "without imposing on others." It also has kept him from pursuing the career he had intended. Mr. Van Dyck has a master's degree in music and taught vocal music in an elementary school for a while but found that his pain and the attendant drain on his energy made it impossible for him to keep up the regular schedule necessary for teaching. He finally returned to his small hometown and now is a church organist and choir director and also works part-time in the public library.

When ankylosing spondylitis does bend a person over so far that he cannot see ahead, surgeons can sometimes perform a high-risk operation called an *osteotomy*, in which they cut across the fused bone, surgically fracturing the spine, in order to straighten it. No operation, however, can rid Mr. Van Dyck of his near-constant pain. He claims, however, that he is not bitter about the disease that life has dealt him.

Spinal Stenosis

In recent years, physicians have become increasingly aware that some backaches and other back problems are caused by a condition they call *spinal stenosis*. The word "stenosis" means a narrowing of any kind. Spinal stenosis can be the narrowing of the central spinal canal, a condition that is called central spinal stenosis and is depicted in the illustration below. In this drawing, abnormal bony growths on two lumbar vertebrae have narrowed the diameter of the spinal canal so much that it squeezes the nerves inside it (shown in rust), which are part of the cauda equina. Above and below this narrowed portion of the spinal canal, the cauda equina remains normal and not squeezed.

Or spinal stenosis also can be the narrowing of an intervertebral foramen. This is called lateral spinal stenosis, and in this case, the constriction would compress or stretch a nerve root.

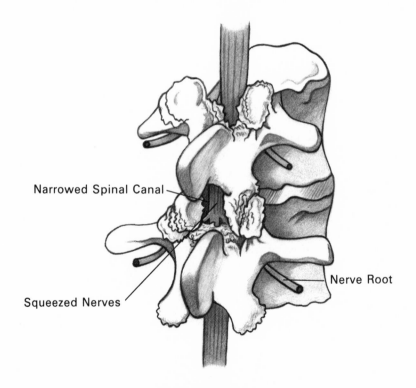

SPINAL STENOSIS

Such narrowings may be due to an injury, to spondylolisthesis (page 86) or to congenital variations in the size and shape of the spinal canal and vertebrae. The most common cause of spinal stenosis, however, is degenerative arthritis, in which the formation of osteophytes can markedly change the contours of our vertebrae.

What spinal stenosis feels like to the afflicted person varies enormously depending upon where it occurs, the specific nerve roots it may affect, and whether or not it presses upon the spinal cord. In the neck, it can produce tingling and numbness in the arms. In the lumbar area, it can produce the characteristic shooting pain of sciatica. It frequently causes leg pains that develop as a person walks and become so intense that he or she must stop. Mrs. Jane Davis, who was mentioned earlier in this chapter, had pains in her hips and legs over a period of two years. At first the pains were on her left side and down the front of her left leg. Then later the pains switched sides and went down her right leg. This leg was also numb. "When I shaved my legs," she recalls, "I had no feelings whatsoever along this side. And I'd stub my toes a lot. I didn't realize I didn't have my foot picked up to walk."

Mrs. Davis was taking pain-relieving drugs, and at one point her physician suggested she try bed rest at home for a week, but neither treatment solved the problem. A myelogram showed that she had lateral spinal stenosis in her lumbar region that was interfering with several different nerve roots on both sides. She underwent surgery to enlarge the narrowed openings and relieve the pressure on those nerves.

Osteoporosis

Osteoporosis, like degenerative arthritis, is also a disease of aging, a condition that most of us will probably develop if we live long enough. *Osteo-* means bone, and *-porosis* comes from the same word roots as porous. Osteoporosis thus means porous bone. As mentioned earlier, the body is constantly building up new bone and destroying old. After a person reaches his or her forties, however, the body gradually begins destroying old bone faster than it rebuilds new bone. As he or she ages, this process results in the bones becoming softer and more porous. The bone we have is normal; we just have less of it. If you think of bone as analogous to Swiss cheese, then in osteoporosis, the bones develop bigger and bigger holes. In severe cases, the holes become so big that the bones may become nearly invisible on x-rays.

According to the National Institute of Arthritis, Diabetes, and Digestive and Kidney Diseases, osteoporosis affects an estimated 15 to 20 million Americans, a number bound to increase in future years as the proportion of older people in our population increases. Osteoporosis also affects women two to four times more frequently than it does men. In some women, it develops particularly rapidly following menopause. Studies of 2,063 women living in southeastern Michigan have dramatically demonstrated the relationship between osteoporosis and aging. Among the women aged forty-five to fifty-four, 39 percent had evidence of osteoporosis on x-rays of their vertebrae. Among those aged fifty-five to sixty-four, 61 percent had it. Of those aged sixty-five to seventy-four, 77 percent had it, and of those over seventy-five, 90 percent had it.

While most of us will eventually develop some osteoporosis, most of us probably will not have any medical problems because of it. The loss of bone in itself is not painful. The significance of osteoporosis is that it makes the bones so brittle they break easily. Osteoporosis is the underlying cause of many of the fractured wrists, arms, ankles and hips that elderly people so commonly suffer. In the spine, osteoporosis makes the vertebrae so fragile that they often collapse under the weight of the upper body, the vertebral bodies crushing down in front so that they become wedge-shaped. In the illustration opposite, the enlarged "window" into the woman's spine shows three vertebrae; the center one has been fractured in this manner, while the vertebrae above and below it remain normal. This is called a compression or crush fracture of a vertebra, and it most frequently occurs in the lower thoracic or upper lumbar regions of the spinal column. In one x-ray survey of 136 otherwise healthy residents of a home for the aged in Philadelphia, 20 percent of the men and 29 percent of the women were found to have such compression fractures of one or more vertebrae. When such a fracture occurs, it also causes a person's spine to angle sharply forward at that point, producing a visible deformity that physicians call a kyphosis (see page 81) and that laymen commonly call a dowager's hump. Such compression fractures are among the several reasons why people so often lose height as they age. In extreme cases, so many vertebrae may collapse that the person's ribs may come to rest on his or her hip-bones.

When such a vertebral fracture occurs, it may cause considerable pain to the person, but it can also happen without that person even being aware of it. Mrs. Marjorie Fellows, for instance, a smartly dressed and carefully coiffed woman in her early sixties, has known

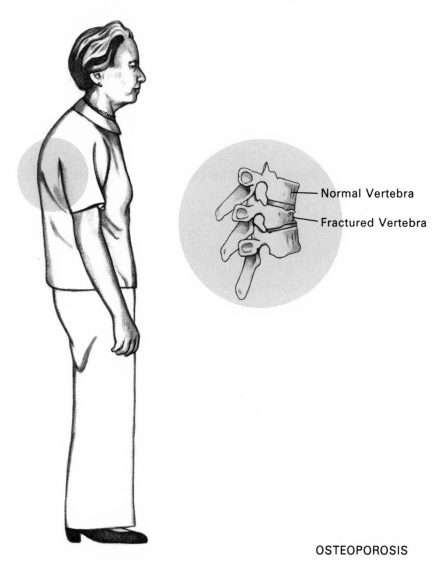

Normal Vertebra

Fractured Vertebra

OSTEOPOROSIS

since she was in her forties, well before her menopause, that she had osteoporosis. She was astonished, however, to learn recently from her doctor that an x-ray showed that she had fractured one of the vertebrae in her lower thoracic region; the front of it had crushed down so far that it was only half the height of the rear portion. The only incident she can recall that might have caused it was a particularly strenuous bout of housecleaning about four years earlier, when she and her husband had learned at the last minute that they were about to have unexpected weekend houseguests. "These people had never been to my house to stay before," Mrs. Fellows explains, "and she's a Mrs. Clean. So I tore into that house. I carried a stepladder around and I washed windows. Afterwards I was in terrific pain for several days, and I haven't been the same since." While Mrs. Fellows did not know she had fractured a vertebra, she had realized that she had lost two inches in height.

Even when a compression fracture is so painful that the person does know something has happened, the fracture does not need to be set in a cast the way a fractured arm or leg would be. Doctors may merely prescribe pain-relieving drugs and recommend that the person rest in bed or wear an orthopedic corset just until the pain subsides.

While osteoporosis is, like degenerative arthritis, a disease of aging, there is also far more to its development than aging alone. Why, for instance, do some people develop the disease at a younger age—in their forties, for example—while others never develop it at all? While medical scientists cannot yet fully answer this question, this is a very active area of research, and many factors have been identified. Scientists now believe that osteoporosis is not a single disease but the end result of many different disorders. It can be a side effect of a number of other diseases and also of many drugs. It can be caused, at least in animals, by a chronic gross deficiency of calcium in the diet. Some people who do get enough calcium from their food, however, may have an impaired ability to absorb the mineral in their intestines or otherwise to utilize it properly. The fact that so many women develop osteoporosis rapidly after menopause seems to indicate that a lack of the female sex hormone estrogen is a major causative factor in women.

Inactivity and lack of exercise may also cause osteoporosis; people who must be bedridden lose bone at a rate faster than normal. Apparently our bones need the pull and tug of the muscles upon them in order to remain healthy. Despite vigorous exercise programs, astronauts living in the weightlessness of space also lose calcium from their bones rapidly enough to cause scientists to fear that some of them might develop significant osteoporosis on the years-long space flights necessary to reach Mars and the other planets.

No treatment now known can reverse the bone loss of osteoporosis, but several measures we all can take may help prevent it. We can all make sure that we get enough calcium in our food. The 1980 edition of the *Recommended Dietary Allowances,* written by the Food and Nutrition Board of the National Research Council and published by the National Academy of Sciences, officially recommends 800 milligrams (about one-fortieth of an ounce) of calcium a day for adults—about the amount contained in two-thirds of a quart of milk, the most common source of calcium in the American diet. Other foods rich in calcium include cheese and other dairy products and dark green leafy vegetables such as spinach. For people known to have osteoporosis, physicians often prescribe calcium supplements. We can all also make sure that we get enough exercise and other physical activity to keep the bones from softening due to disuse.

Estrogen, the female sex hormone, can help prevent osteoporosis, at least in some women, but its use poses other serious problems. For years physicians had prescribed estrogens for women to prevent the discomforting hot flushes and other symptoms of menopause, but it was not then known whether estrogen could also prevent osteoporosis. In 1975, however, several new studies showed that women taking estrogen have a greater risk of developing cancer of the endometrium (the lining of the uterus), and the use of estrogen dropped sharply. Now subsequent studies have demonstrated that estrogen does indeed retard the bone loss of osteoporosis, and the Food and Drug Administration (FDA) is weighing approval of the use of estrogen for this purpose. The FDA stresses, however, that estrogen should be used only together with a good general diet, calcium supplements and sufficient exercise, and that women taking estrogen should be checked regularly by their doctor for signs of cancer.

Nevertheless, many questions about estrogens still remain unanswered. One, according to Dr. Solomon Sobel, M.D., director of the FDA's Division of Metabolism and Endocrine Drug Products, is whether estrogen use actually decreases the number of bone fractures. "We don't have a very good study showing that." Who should take estrogens? With the increased risk of endometrial cancer, Dr. Sobel points out, "we obviously don't want to recommend that all women take estrogens in the hopes of treating those 20 percent who otherwise would develop severe osteoporosis. But we don't have a good way to identify the women who are good candidates. Family history might be an indicator, if a sister or other close relative has severe osteoporosis. Or do we wait for a bone fracture?" If a woman has had a hysterectomy (the surgical removal of the uterus), she runs no risk of endometrial cancer and a physician would be more likely to prescribe estrogen. How long should a woman take estrogens? "And if one stops estrogens, will there be an accelerated bone loss so that the amount of bone loss would soon be the same as if the woman had never taken estrogens? We don't have the studies to tell us."

There is also ongoing scientific research on several other drugs that may or may not ultimately prove useful in preventing osteoporosis. Some of these other drugs could also be taken by the many men who have osteoporosis.

People with osteoporosis who have already had one compression fracture of a vertebra run a great risk of fracturing another vertebra. For this reason, Mrs. Fellows has learned to be very, very careful of her back. She has long taken calcium supplements, and her doctor tells her that she must be as active as possible without stressing her spine, walking for exercise. Mrs. Fellows has given up golf and also housecleaning because she finds them too strenuous. She is so apprehensive about the car hitting any bumps that her husband lets her do the driving. "I don't dare fall," Mrs. Fellows notes sadly. "The doctor said just treat my back like it's an eggshell."

Scoliosis

Sixteen-year-old Karen, a long-legged, willowy high school junior, shows off the heavy custom-made orthopedic brace she has worn for the last three years. A stiff form-fitting girdle encircles her hips. From it, three upright metal bars—one in front and two in back—run up to a padded ring around her neck that fits, at the rear, snugly under her skull. On her right side, another padded part presses against her back. This cumbersome contraption, gently stretching and straightening Karen's torso as she has grown over these years, has kept her from developing an ugly, lifelong and potentially crippling deformity of her spine. The brace is a new treatment that has become available only in the last generation or so.

Karen has *scoliosis* (the Greek word for crookedness), which is a sideways curvature of the spine. Poor posture, a short leg, or a sideways tilt of the hips can cause a spinal curvature flexible enough to permit a person to straighten it out at will. In true structural scoliosis, like Karen's, however, the person cannot straighten out the curvature because it is produced by abnormal shapes of the bones, as is shown in the illustration on page 80. The vertebrae themselves are deformed, both bent to one side and twisted, and the ribs are also misshapen, crowded closer together on one side (on the left in the girl in the drawing) and spread apart and pushed toward the rear on the other side, forming a hump. If the girl in the illustration bent forward, you would be able to see a distinct hump on the right side of her upper back.

Because scoliosis is so conspicuous, it must have been among the earliest back diseases recognized. Stone Age artists depicted scoliosis in their cave paintings, and a pair of pottery figures fashioned by Indians in what is now Mexico, long before Columbus arrived in the New World, show a man and a woman with their spines twisted into sharp S curves. From ancient times, physicians have tried—with little success until recently—ingenious devices for straightening out such curves: padded, racklike apparatuses; metal plates forged by armorers; and in the nineteenth century, casts made from plaster of paris.

Physicians now know that many things can cause a structural scoliosis: injury, infection and certain other diseases such as cerebral

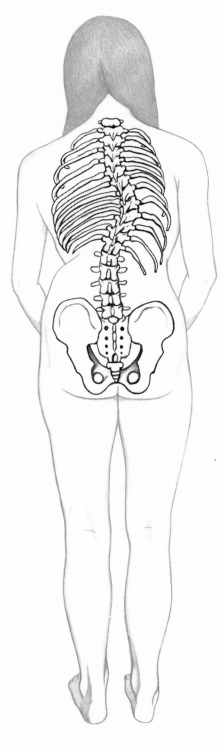

SCOLIOSIS

palsy and muscular dystrophy. Before the introduction of the polio vaccine in the mid-1950s, poliomyelitis used to cause many such spinal curvatures. In most cases of scoliosis, however, there is no known cause. Physicians call this idiopathic scoliosis. (The word "idiopathic" means of an unknown cause.) There is, however, a strong hereditary factor. Like so many diseases, scoliosis tends to run in families; for example, both Karen's mother and grandmother have it.

Scoliosis usually first becomes apparent as a child enters his or her second decade of life, at the same time as he or she begins the rapid growth of adolescence. Within a few short years a curvature—if not treated—can rapidly become much more severe, tilting a person sideways until the shoulders are grotesquely aslant. While scoliosis is not necessarily painful, it can, because the spine is so out of balance, lead to severe degenerative arthritis later in life. The misshapen ribs may also reduce the capacity of the lungs and press upon the heart, causing respiratory and cardiac disease serious enough to shorten a person's life. Unfortunately, there is no way to tell until it is too late for preventive bracing whether a given adolescent's scoliosis is going to get worse, and if so, how much worse.

It was not until recent years that physicians finally developed an effective nonsurgical treatment for scoliosis. During the 1950s and 1960s, Walter P. Blount, M.D., of the Medical College of Wisconsin in Milwaukee developed the removable brace that Karen wears, known as the Milwaukee brace. He discovered that if adolescents with scoliosis wore this brace all during their growing years, it, combined with an exercise program, would—in most cases—keep the curvature from becoming worse. Today there are other newer types of braces that are also in widespread use. With this preventive treatment now available, it is important that children's curvatures be spotted early, while they are still slight. Many school districts now routinely inspect children for early signs of scoliosis. Typically, a school nurse or a physical education teacher trained by a physician checks the children in the fifth through tenth grades, usually once a year.

These school screening programs also look for signs of another type of spinal curvature called *kyphosis* (from the Greek word for humpback). Kyphosis is an abnormal forward curvature of the spine, also called *hunchback* or *roundback*. This condition, which also must have been recognized by our prehistoric ancestors, is depicted in art and literature. A humpback is the hero of both a French novel (Victor Hugo's *Hunchback of Notre Dame*) and an Italian opera (Giuseppe Verdi's *Rigoletto*). Kyphosis, too, can have many causes: injury, infection and other diseases. It can be congenital; Victor Hugo tells us that his fictional hunchback was born that way. Kyphosis used to be a common result of spinal tuberculosis. In older people, it can be caused by osteoporosis, as was mentioned earlier in this chapter. And like scoliosis, it can also develop in growing children for unknown reasons. This kind of developmental kyphosis is often called Scheuermann's disease, after the German physician who first discovered, in 1920, that it is due to misshapen vertebrae. While kyphosis is less common than scoliosis, it can be even more serious. In very severe cases, which are usually congenital or due to injury or infection, this forward curvature can press against the spinal cord and cause paralysis. In recent decades, however, physicians have also improved preventive bracing and surgical techniques for kyphosis, and it is important to spot these forward curvatures too, while they are still slight. If the school your children attend does not have a scoliosis and kyphosis screening program, you can easily examine your children's spine periodically for these curvatures yourself. See the box on page 84 for instructions.

The school screening programs, according to the Scoliosis Research Society, find some signs of scoliosis in as many as 4 percent of children between the ages of ten and fourteen. The schools recommend that parents have these children evaluated by their family physician. About half of these children, about 2 percent, then require treatment or continued observation by a physician. The screening programs detect scoliosis equally frequently in boys and girls, but for unknown reasons, it is more likely to become severe in girls. Of those who do need treatment, 80 percent are girls.

Karen was ten years old and going into fifth grade when her family doctor first noticed that she, like her mother and grandmother, was developing some sideways curvature of her spine. He referred her to a specialist. A series of x-rays revealed that between her eighth and eleventh thoracic vertebrae her spine was curving toward the right, but not enough so to require that she start wearing a brace. She was, however, to return to the specialist every three months for more x-rays on which he would, each time, as she grew, measure her curvature.

Karen visited the specialist regularly during fifth, sixth and seventh grades. Then toward the end of seventh grade, she was told by her doctor that her curve, as measured on her x-rays, was getting worse. He described the Milwaukee brace to her and explained that if she wore this brace throughout her teens it probably could prevent her curve from increasing.

Karen was understandably upset at the prospect. She feared her friends would drop her. "I didn't want to have it," she recalls, "and before I got it, I cried a lot. I was scared." But Karen had underestimated her friends. The first day she came home wearing the brace, she hid in her room. When her friends came over and tried to persuade her to go out with them, "I told them I didn't want anybody to see me. But they said, 'You're not any different.' And they made me go with them." Her parents, too, "were really good," she says, insisting that she go places and do things. Karen had tried to resign from the cheerleading squad when she learned about the brace, but again, the leaders "made me jump, made me get on top of pyramids." In gym, Karen found she could do everything but tumble.

At first Karen wore the brace nearly twenty-four hours a day; she was allowed out of it only for quick showers. And every day she had to do special exercises in her brace. She also had to return to the doctor every three months for more x-rays to monitor what was happening with her curvature, and also for adjustments to the brace as she grew taller. Karen wore her brace constantly throughout the eighth and ninth grades. It became "just part of me," she says; she even gave it a nickname, "Tilly." During tenth grade, Karen was doing so well that she was allowed to remain out of the brace several hours a day, and now, a year later, as she enters eleventh grade, she wears it only at night.

If Karen's parents had not seen to it that she wore a brace, or if the brace had not held her curvature, she might have needed surgery. The first fusion for scoliosis was not done until 1914, when Russell A. Hibbs, M.D., of New York City fused the spine of a boy

HOW PARENTS SHOULD INSPECT CHILDREN FOR SCOLIOSIS AND KYPHOSIS

If your children's school does not screen students for scoliosis and kyphosis, it is simple for you to do it yourself at home. Have your child's back bare at least from the waist up —a boy dressed only in shorts, and a girl in panties or shorts and bra or bathing-suit top—so that you can see the back clearly. First, have the child simply stand naturally and look at him or her carefully from the front, rear and side for the signs listed below. Then have the child bend over in the position shown in the illustration opposite, and again look carefully from the front, rear and side.

Do you see any of the following possible signs of scoliosis or kyphosis?

• Is there any noticeable asymmetry or evidence of lack of proportion?
• Is one shoulder notably higher than the other?
• Is one shoulder blade notably more prominent than the other?
• In girls, are the breasts noticeably asymmetrical?
• Is the waistline noticeably higher or indented farther on one side than the other?
• Is one hip noticeably higher than the other?
• When the child is standing straight, is there considerably more space between the arm and the body on one side than the other?
• Is there an obvious sideways curve to the spine?
• Is there any hump on the back? This may become more visible when the child is bending over as in the illustration.

If you see any of these signs, consult your family doctor.

CHECKING FOR SCOLIOSIS AND KYPHOSIS

who had scoliosis due to polio. In 1962, Paul R. Harrington, M.D., of Baylor University College of Medicine in Houston devised an instrument—called the Harrington rod—that now forms the basis of most modern scoliosis surgery. The Harrington rod is a slender steel structure that surgeons can implant next to the backbone along the entire length of the curvature—perhaps as many as thirteen vertebrae—hooking it into the spine to straighten out the curvature as much as possible. Next, they fuse together all of the deformed vertebrae, which are held straight by the rod as they heal into a single, solid mass. Such surgery is an extensive procedure. The person operated upon also must wear a body cast for nine months or so and is left with a portion of the spine permanently stiff.

Karen is now upset not at the idea of wearing the brace for years but at people with scoliosis who won't undergo this preventive treatment. Karen knows another girl with even more of a curvature than hers who refuses to wear a brace. "I tell her that she is going to have a lot of trouble when she gets older, but she just says, 'Oh, that's life.' I hate that."

Spondylolisthesis

In spite of its difficult name *spondylolisthesis* (pronounced spon″-dĭ-lo-lis′-the-sis) is a fairly straightforward structural disease of the spine. *Spondyl-* comes from the Greek word for vertebra, and *-olisthesis* from the Greek word for slip. Spondylolisthesis thus means slipped vertebra, and that is exactly what this back disease is. As noted earlier in this chapter, the term "slipped disc" is a misnomer for a herniated disc; our intervertebral discs cannot slip out of place. Yet our vertebrae can on occasion do just that.

In Chapter 1 it was mentioned that the weight-bearing surfaces of our vertebrae—contrary to what one would expect—do not generally lie horizontally—that is, parallel to the ground. Most of them lie at a distinct slant, and the upper surface of the sacrum in particular slopes, on the average, nearly 45 degrees, as shown in the illustration. This tilted surface of the sacrum helps set the stage for spondylolisthesis.

A normal, intact vertebra, however, could not slip. The small facet joints at its rear firmly lock it to the vertebra below. For slippage to occur, the vertebra must be defective, with a crack across it in such a way that the rear portion of the vertebra, with its facet joints, is detached from the front portion. Such a defect is called *spondylolysis* (*spondyl-*, again, from the Greek word for vertebra, and *-olysis* from the word for dissolve or loosen). The cause of such a crack seems to be some hereditary weakness combined with prolonged mechanical stresses, which gradually produce what physicians call a fatigue fracture.

If a person has this crack, it is possible for it slowly to widen (as is shown in the illustration below) under the weight of the upper body, allowing the detached front portion of the vertebra gradually to slip on the vertebra below. In most cases it is the lowermost lumbar vertebra, as shown here, that slides down the sloping upper surface of the sacrum, distorting the intervening disc and carrying along with it the entire upper spinal column.

Such spondylolisthesis is one back disease that seems to be unique to our human species. No other animal is known to develop it quite in this way, points out Leon L. Wiltse, M.D., of Memorial Hospital Medical Center in Long Beach, California, who for many years has made a special study of this disease. Four-footed animals, with hori-

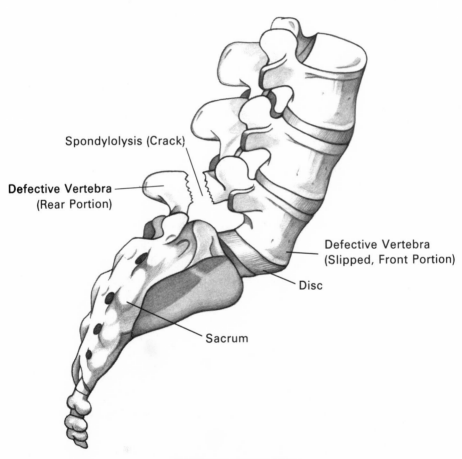

Spondylolysis (Crack)

Defective Vertebra
(Rear Portion)

Defective Vertebra
(Slipped, Front Portion)

Disc

Sacrum

SPONDYLOLISTHESIS

zontal spines, do not experience this exact sort of slippage, nor do even our closest relatives, the great apes. Human spondylolisthesis thus does seem to be caused in part by our upright posture. Only in humans does the weight of the upper body chronically press upon the lower spine, where—once the crack occurs—it can impel the downward slippage characteristic of spondylolisthesis.

Physicians have recognized spondylolisthesis for a least two centuries. In 1782, a Belgian obstetrician noticed patients with slippage so great it interfered with childbirth. Not until after the widespread introduction of x-ray diagnosis during the early part of this century, however, were physicians able to learn much about the condition.

The underlying defect (spondylolysis), which is harmless in itself, is surprisingly common; about one out of twenty of us has this crack across the back of our lowermost lumbar vertebra. In some population groups, the prevalence of this defect is even higher, notably among some Eskimos in northern Alaska. In one x-ray survey of 153 northern Eskimos admitted to the Alaska Native Service Hospital in Anchorage for reasons other than back problems, researchers found that 28 percent of them had the crack.

Only in about half the people with the crack, however, does any slippage occur, according to studies by Dr. Wiltse, and in most of these people it usually does not produce any significant symptoms. "There are probably many people with this condition who don't know they have it and never have any trouble from it," says Dr. Wiltse. "And we don't actually know what percentage of people who do have it develop enough pain to cause them to see a doctor. But among people with back pain severe enough to consult a doctor, this is a fairly common cause of the pain."

Most people with backaches from spondylolisthesis are able to keep it under control by conservative means—bed rest and pain-relieving drugs when pain is bad; wearing an orthopedic corset at times; and exercising after the pain subsides to strengthen the abdominal muscles supporting the spine. A small minority, however, may have so much trouble that they ultimately need surgery.

Lloyd Eagleton, for instance, is a compact, dark-haired man who began having aches in his lower back when he was a teenager. In his twenties, he recalls, they became "terrible" at times. He worked in a meat-packing plant, and his job at the time involved heavy lifting. He was constantly bruising his lower back and getting "sharp pains back there, which eventually would go down to a steady ache." When he was x-rayed at work, he recalls being told "that I had a misalignment there, that the vertebrae were not lined up. It was a defect in my back I would have to live with." He had noticed he had "a dip in the small of the back you could lay your thumb in. It was really caved in." About that time he happened to change his particular job within the plant, and his back started to feel better.

When Mr. Eagleton was in his mid-thirties, however, he began to experience numbness in his legs, "down through the thigh, through the knee, down into the ankle." While he was driving on vacation one spring, his right leg and foot—the one on the gas pedal —would go numb. "It continued to get worse. At work, I'd have to sit down sometimes to relieve the pain and numbness. Later, it got so sitting wasn't comfortable, and I'd have to get up and move around to relieve it. Soon it got so I couldn't climb stairs." He tried heat treatments and wearing an orthopedic corset, but they did not help enough.

Finally, that fall, he visited a specialist, who for the first time told him that he had spondylolisthesis and that in his case the defective vertebra was pinching nerves in his lower back. "He told me that the pain might get worse and that the solution was to undergo surgery. 'You can have your surgery now,' he told me, 'or you can wait. It's up to you. Eventually you will probably have to have something done.' "

Mr. Eagleton pondered this advice and then the next month did undergo surgery to fuse his slipping vertebra to the one below. This meant spending three months in a long body cast, and being off work for six months. Since he is now a supervisor, he no longer does heavy physical work on his job. "There is always some strain there, and still some tingling and a little bit of numbness, but I feel fortunate to be able to lead a normal life. I can do just about anything I want to do. It seems as solid as a bolt back there, probably stronger than it's ever been."

Congenital Anomalies

The illustrations of the human spine in Chapter 1 depict the anatomy of the average adult. Actually, our backbones vary so much in the details of their conformation that about half of us, it is estimated, have some congenital anomaly of the vertebrae—most of them minor and quite innocuous. About 20 percent of us have some departure from the normal formula for the number of vertebrae in

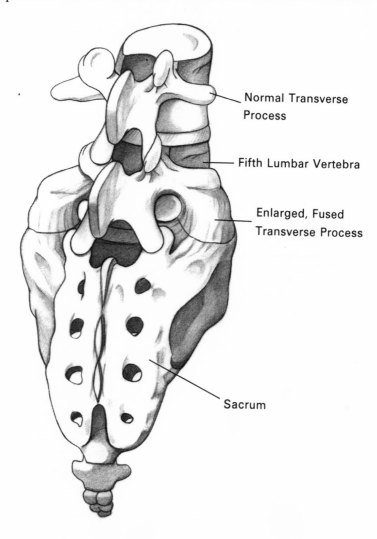

Normal Transverse
Process

Fifth Lumbar Vertebra

Enlarged, Fused
Transverse Process

Sacrum

FUSED FIFTH LUMBAR VERTEBRA

each region of the spine: neck, seven; thoracic, twelve; lumbar, five; sacral, five (fused); and coccyx, four (fused). The coccyx often has three or five vertebrae instead of four. Some people have an extra rib attached to the lowermost neck or uppermost lumbar vertebra (the so-called gorilla rib), giving them in effect an extra chest verte-bra. Many people have some anomaly of the lowermost (fifth) lum-bar vertebra or sacrum. The sacrum may have only four fused vertebrae, with what would otherwise be the topmost sacral vertebra separate, forming an extra or sixth lumbar vertebra. Physicians dis-agree about whether such an extra lumbar vertebra makes a person more prone to backaches. Or, conversely, the fifth lumbar vertebra may be fused to the sacrum (as shown in the illustration opposite). The transverse processes on either side are enlarged and bend down-ward to form two bony bridges with the sacrum, thus reducing the number of free lumbar vertebrae to four. Such a fused fifth lumbar vertebra occurs in about 1 percent of the population and probably does not, most physicians believe, make a person more susceptible to back pain. Indeed, it probably strengthens the lumbar region.

Another common anatomical variant is one commonly known as a "hole in the spine," shown in the illustration below. Sometimes a vertebra fails to form completely, and the bony ring, which nor-mally encircles the spinal canal, has a small gap in it at the rear. This gap is usually filled with scar tissue. Physicians call this anomaly a *spina bifida occulta*, a Latin phrase meaning hidden two-part spine. Such a hole in the spine occurs, it is variously estimated, in 5 to 10 percent of the population and is rarely of any significance at all.

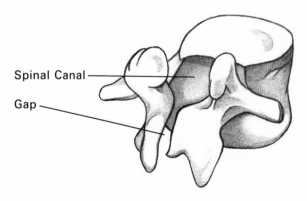

Spinal Canal

Gap

"HOLE IN THE SPINE"

Another anatomical variant often blamed for back pain is a short leg—that is, a person having one leg slightly shorter than the other. A large discrepancy between leg lengths could well cause backache because of the uneven stress on muscles and other tissues. However, most physicians believe that a difference of half an inch or less is probably insignificant.

Fortunately, catastrophic congenital defects of the spine—unlike those of the heart—are rare. The most serious and the most common is a more extreme version of the innocuous hole in the spine described above. Sometimes as a fetus develops, a vertebra forms so poorly that it has an even larger gap at its rear; some of the contents of the spinal canal—the meninges covering the spinal cord and the spinal cord itself—may protrude through this large gap, forming a bulge on the baby's back that is conspicuous at birth. Confusingly, this serious condition is called by a Latin name very similar to that of the innocuous version: *spina bifida* or *spina bifida with meningomyelocele.* According to the U.S. Public Health Service's Birth Defects Monitoring Program, spina bifida occurs in about 5 out of every 10,000 births. It is one of the most serious emergency situations that can become evident at childbirth. Such babies usually need immediate neurological surgery and then also require continuing costly medical, surgical and rehabilitative care throughout their lives. Even then most of them are partially paralyzed, and many are also mentally retarded, because of an associated birth defect called hydrocephalus (literally, "water-brain"). Ironically, by saving the lives of babies who previously would have died, modern medicine (antibiotics and improved surgical techniques) has significantly increased the number of people crippled by spina bifida. The Food and Drug Administration is weighing approval of a blood test, already in use for several years in Great Britain, that could be administered to any pregnant woman to help assess the likelihood of her unborn child having this disastrous birth defect.

There are also several other more subtle birth defects of the spine and spinal cord that may gradually cause significant neurological trouble as a child grows. An errant bit of bone, for instance, may impale and tether the spinal cord or the cauda equina so that muscles fail to develop properly or become partially paralyzed. Such concealed malformations often reveal themselves by certain telltale signs on the child's skin, on the midline of the back overlying the defect: a patch of hair, a dimple or an opening, a fatty tumor or a reddish birthmark. Alert obstetricians and pediatricians usually routinely inspect newborn babies for such external signs of these internal defects.

Infections

Among the many back diseases that can cause back pain are infections with some sort of microorganism: bacteria or, less commonly, a fungus. Such infections are more common among children and elderly people, and are often accompanied by a high fever and also by more pain than most backaches. While infections are not now among the most common causes of back pain in the United States, when they do occur, the particular offending organism should be identified as promptly as possible so that appropriate antibiotic or other treatment can begin.

The most common infecting organism used to be the tuberculosis bacillus, which would sometimes invade the spinal column from the bloodstream. This *spinal tuberculosis* is also called Pott's disease, after Sir Percival Pott of Great Britain, who first described the disease in 1779. Until relatively recently Pott's disease was a major crippler of children. It can eat away the vertebrae and cause them to collapse, leaving the child with a lifelong kyphosis. Then, in the early twentieth century, better sanitation, including the pasteurization of milk, and, in the mid-1940s and early 1950s, the introduction of antituberculosis drugs dramatically reduced the incidence of tuberculosis. According to the U.S. Public Health Service's Center for Disease Control, by the early 1980s the number of cases of tuberculosis was down below 13 per 100,000 people, less than 28,000 cases altogether. In other, less developed countries, however, particularly in Africa and Asia, Pott's disease and the deformities it can cause are still common.

In this country, today, the microorganism that most often causes spinal infection is *Staphylococcus aureus,* a bacterium frequently found on the surface of the skin. Among drug addicts, spinal infections are more commonly caused by a different bacterium, *Pseudomonas.* Infections of the spine can come about in strange ways, and they often can be very difficult to diagnose. Charlie Hobbs, for instance, a trim, dark-blond college junior, had a slight backache one day in late summer, but he had played four games of basketball the day before "to get in shape." That night, however, he couldn't sleep, and by morning, he recalls, "it was all I could do to walk over to the student health center." Over the next two weeks, Charlie became sick enough that he could not attend classes and eventually went home, some forty miles away. His temperature reached 104 degrees; he had a "terrible pain in the middle of my back. My stomach muscles were just in a constant spasm, constantly tight, and I couldn't walk very well or very fast." During these weeks he consulted three different physicians without finding what was wrong. Finally one of the physicians referred Charlie to a specialist, an orthopedist, who hospitalized him. X-rays showed that Charlie had an abnormally narrowed intervertebral disc near the base of his thoracic region, and a more sophisticated diagnostic test called a *bone scan* showed that he also had a hot spot—a place where new bone was being formed (and, by implication, where bone was also being destroyed). Such a hot spot could be caused by a number of different diseases. Next, with Charlie under a general anesthetic in an operating room, the orthopedist performed a *needle biopsy:* he inserted a long, sturdy, hollow needle into the hot-spot area of Charlie's spine and withdrew some fluid and tissue. Laboratory analysis of this material revealed that Charlie had a spinal infection caused by the common bacterium *Staphylococcus aureus.*

How did this bacterium travel from Charlie's skin, its normal habitat, into his backbone? The orthopedist and he both believe that its journey started months earlier, from an unusually large blister on his heel which had developed during a strenuous eight-day skiing expedition in the Colorado wilderness. The blister had been so severe that Charlie felt terrible and had had to spend one day in camp. One of the group leaders on the trip had drained the blister for Charlie and, he says, "everything was hunky-dory for eight months." But apparently the *Staphylococcus* had gotten into his body at that time and entered his bloodstream.

With the organism causing the infection identified, the orthopedist treated Charlie by putting him in a lightweight plastic body cast to immobilize the area so that the infection could heal itself. Using this, Charlie was able to go back to college after five days in the hospital. Although his back was still somewhat painful, he could walk around and even found that he could still press weights to keep in shape. He wore the cast for two months, and then an orthopedic corset for a while. "At least I knew what was wrong," he says. "When I realized that there was a good chance there wouldn't be anything wrong with me long term, I was so relieved."

Fractures

A person can break any vertebra of the back from the atlas to the coccyx. Yet as noted in Chapter 1, fractures do not occur randomly along the spine. They most frequently happen in two specific locations, as shown in rust in the illustration on page 96: in three vertebrae above the waist (the two lowermost chest vertebrae and the uppermost lumbar one), and to a lesser extent in the three lowermost neck vertebrae. These locations seem to be determined by the structural characteristics of the spine. Both are junctions between the more flexible regions of the spine (the neck and lumbar regions) and the more rigid thoracic region, which is stiffened by the ribs. When the spinal column receives a back-breaking blow or is suddenly whipped back and forth, the stress is concentrated at these two junctions.

A broken backbone can be one of the most catastrophic of all accidents. The jagged pieces of bone or other injured tissue can severely compress or even sever the spinal cord, rendering a person permanently paralyzed from the site of the injury down to the toes. If the spinal cord is cut at the neck, it can kill the person instantly or turn him or her into a quadriplegic, unable to move and without any feelings in the arms, torso or legs. If the spinal cord is cut near the waist, it can leave the person a paraplegic, unable to move and without any feelings in the lower torso or legs. Because of this great danger, do *not* move anyone who has been injured and may have broken his or her back. (For instructions on what to do if you are faced with this situation, see box on page 97.)

Ironically, modern medicine has also significantly increased the number of paraplegic and quadriplegic people in our society by saving the lives (with antibiotics, improved surgical methods and

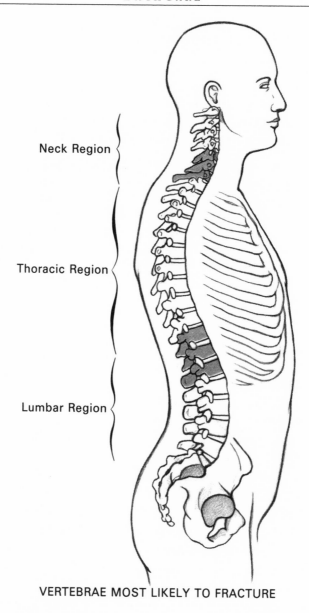

Neck Region

Thoracic Region

Lumbar Region

VERTEBRAE MOST LIKELY TO FRACTURE

better overall care) of people who previously would have died. Such catastrophic back injuries most often happen to young men between the ages of sixteen and thirty-five, and are most frequently the result of motor vehicle accidents. There are more than 10,000 new spinal cord injuries in the United States each year, and according to the National Center for Health Statistics, a total of approximately

WHAT TO DO IN CASE OF A BROKEN BACK

If an accident victim has neck pain, tingling or paralysis in the arms or legs, a head injury, or is unconscious, suspect that he or she may have broken the neck or some other part of the backbone. *Do not move the person.* Any movement could sever the spinal cord and thereby permanently paralyze or even kill the person.

Call for a qualified person—a physician or trained ambulance personnel—and wait for him or her to arrive on the scene to transport the injured person to a hospital for diagnostic x-rays.

If it is absolutely necessary for you to move the victim because of some life-threatening situation—such as drowning or fire—do so very gently and carefully. Do not let the spine bend or twist; keep it in a straight line. Try to find something, such as a board, to which you can tie the person at the head and buttocks to support and immobilize the spine.

If it is essential to drag the person immediately to safety, do so by pulling both arms or both legs to keep the spine as straight as possible. *Do not* drag the person sideways.

—Adapted from the American Medical Association *Handbook of First Aid and Emergency Care*

125,000 paraplegics and quadriplegics altogether. Such people require an enormous amount of continuing care, both for medical problems and also simply to go about their daily lives. The cost of this care can be immense. The Insurance Institute for Highway Safety estimates that each paraplegic or quadriplegic costs over $200,000 each year—$94,000 in direct costs and $110,000 in such indirect costs as the loss of productivity. The overall cost of spinal cord injuries to society, the institute estimates, is over $1.6 billion each year.

Nevertheless, you should not panic if a physician tells you that you have broken your spine. Broken backs range considerably in seriousness. Most of them are not catastrophic, and many are almost inconsequential. If the fracture has done no nerve damage, it may not even need to be set or require wearing a cast. Indeed, as was mentioned earlier in this chapter in the section on osteoporosis, many older people with soft, porous bones have compression fractures of vertebrae without even being aware of it—and with no need for medical care. Due to the potential danger, however, you should assume any broken back is serious until it can be x-rayed and evaluated by a physician.

Sprains and Strains

A sprain is a partial tearing of ligaments (the tough, fibrous structures that bind the bones together at the joints), usually due to an injury. A strain is an overstretching of ligaments and muscles, often due to overexertion. Both sprains and strains signal their presence by pain.

Sprains and strains can be more elusive to diagnose than many more serious back diseases. Such soft-tissue injuries do not generally show on x-rays, which primarily show only bone well. However, physicians can sometimes see muscle spasms in the back or deduce an injury from a person's pattern of pain or stiffness. Other times they may make a diagnosis of a sprain or a strain in the back largely on the basis of the person's history—the backache has developed after an accident or some unaccustomed activity, such as overambitious gardening or sports—plus a process of elimination: that is, diagnostic tests yield no physical evidence of any other injury.

Early in this century physicians often ascribed back pains, particularly sciatica, to a sprain of the ligaments of the sacroiliac joints, between the sacrum and the hipbones on either side. Then after the discovery in the 1930s that many hitherto mysterious backaches were due to herniated intervertebral discs, physicians made the diagnosis of a sacroiliac sprain much less frequently.

Today, physicians disagree about how common sprains and strains of the back actually are. Many doctors believe that sprains and strains are a major cause of backaches. Many others, however, believe that sprains and strains of the ligaments and muscles of the back are not all that common.

Backaches due to sprains and strains, like most backaches, tend to go away spontaneously in a few days or weeks. In the meantime many of them can be relieved, if necessary, by such treatments as bed rest, pain-relieving drugs, and heat and massage.

One specific type of spinal sprain that probably has increased in modern times is acute sprain of the neck—often called a whiplash injury. Typically, a person is riding in a motor vehicle of some sort when it is struck from behind. The automobile or other vehicle suddenly jerks forward, snapping the person's head and neck sharply backward. (This is the injury that high-backed automobile and airplane seats are designed to prevent.) After the accident, the person has persistent neck pain, but x-rays and other tests show no fracture or other physical evidence of injury. Physicians usually treat such neck sprains by having the person wear a soft orthopedic collar for a while, to immobilize the injured tissues and allow them to heal. Such whiplash injuries are often involved in litigation, since the vehicle that struck the other from the rear is usually considered at fault.

Another source of occasional backache is simply muscle tension. Many of us from time to time develop some pain in the upper back, across the shoulders and up the back of the neck, after working a long day at the office or after carrying heavy packages some distance. Much of such neck muscle tension is probably due to psychological stress, and it usually can be relieved by anything that helps us relax: lying down for a few minutes, taking a mild pain reliever, applying heat, or having a friend massage the back of the shoulders and neck.

Tumors

Among the less common but most serious possible causes of back pain or other back trouble are tumors, both benign and malignant. Tumor pain often has a somewhat different character from pain due to other back diseases. Usually more constant and worse at night, it is usually not relieved by rest or by changing the position of the body. If back trouble is caused by a tumor, it is important to identify it promptly so that appropriate treatment—surgery, radiation or chemotherapy—can begin.

Almost any kind of cancer—breast, kidney, lung, prostate—can metastasize to the spine and first reveal itself as a backache. Such cancers are more frequent in older people. Primary tumors of the spinal column itself are rare; the most common malignant one is multiple myeloma, a highly fatal form of cancer that most often strikes people between the ages of fifty and seventy. Several different types of benign tumors of the spine, while not usually fatal, can do a lot of damage unless they are diagnosed and treated without delay.

William Rubin, for instance, is a modish young man in his mid-twenties, a welder by trade, who sports a blond goatee and a mustache. Toward the end of February, Mr. Rubin "started to get some numbness in my toes. Over a three-week period, it worked its way gradually up my legs, and I lost my coordination. I was tripping over stuff. If I wanted to go up a step, I didn't know how high to lift my legs. Finally the numbness went clear up to my waist and —I was playing basketball regularly that winter—it got to the point where I couldn't even run up and down the court. And at work I couldn't do anything."

When Mr. Rubin saw his family physician in mid-March, his doctor immediately referred him to a specialist in the city, thirty miles away, who saw him on an emergency basis and admitted him to the hospital that very day. "He was rapidly becoming paraplegic," the specialist recalls. "It was perfectly obvious something was pressing on his spinal cord. He wasn't able to control the muscles of his legs. He walked with his legs far apart and his toes turned out for stability, the way you see a drunk doing." A spinal infection could do this, and so could a tumor and also certain other diseases. Diagnostic tests, however, yielded no evidence of an infection, and a CAT scan (see page 113) and other tests showed that Mr. Rubin had a chondroma, a rare but benign spinal tumor, in his upper chest. Less than half an inch in diameter, it was squeezing his spinal cord. Mr. Rubin would need immediate neurosurgery at the university medical center seventy-five miles away. In the few hours it took to make arrangements for the trip, the numbness climbed well above his waist, and he also lost control of his bladder and his bowels. At the medical center, he recalls, as he went into surgery, "they gave me a 45 percent chance that I might have some paralysis after I got out."

Now, however, five months after surgery, Mr. Rubin walks perfectly normally, and although he still has some soreness from the surgery, he has been back at work for two months and otherwise feels fine. He is thankful for a narrow escape. "They told me, too, that if I had waited one more week I might be paralyzed right now, because it went that fast." There is still a chance that the chondroma may recur, and he must return periodically to the medical center for a checkup, but, he says, "I'm not losing any sleep over it."

Low Back Pain

Despite the fact that there are so many possible causes of back pain, it not infrequently happens that physicians—given all their diagnostic tools—are unable to pinpoint any specific cause for a given backache in a given person. Such mysterious back pains sometimes occur in the neck, but most often they occur in the low back, the lumbar region, which in the human spine, as we have seen, is subject to so much pressure from the weight of our upper body.

The inability to discover a specific physical cause for a given backache does not necessarily mean that a cause does not exist or that the pain is not real. Even the most sophisticated diagnostic methods cannot detect everything that happens inside a body structure as complex as the back, particularly as we bend and twist and lift in the course of daily work and play. Nor is it useless to have undergone a long series of diagnostic tests that in the end uncover nothing wrong. At least one then knows that one does not need specific treatment for any of the identifiable back diseases discussed in this chapter.

Some physicians believe that the most common causes of these undiagnosable back pains are muscular sprains and strains, which, as we noted earlier, often cannot be detected by x-rays or other tests. Many others, however, believe that such backaches are usually due to incipient disease of the intervertebral discs. These physicians note that many people suffer from intermittent mysterious backaches over a period of years and then ultimately do develop obvious herniated discs. Apparently, the earlier pain was produced by some slight tear of the annulus or some subtle bulge of the disc preceding the final, frank herniation.

In any event, such elusive back pains, like so many backaches, do tend to come and go spontaneously, flaring up for a few days or weeks, then subsiding again by themselves. And they too are often relieved by the nonspecific treatments—bed rest, pain-relieving drugs, the application of heat or massage—which will be discussed in detail in Chapter 4. These enigmatic backaches are also often alleviated by many of the measures that any of us can take to help the back—which will be discussed in Chapter 5.

Psychological Factors

As in most diseases, particularly chronic ones, psychological factors often play a role in back disease both as cause and effect, sometimes influencing the point at which a person experiences a flare-up of back pain and also a person's reaction to that pain. The human mind and body are so intricately intertwined, however, that it is virtually impossible most of the time to separate these psychological factors from the many physiological factors that are also involved. Many of us seem to have a physiological weak link that tends to break down from time to time when the unavoidable psychological stresses of our lives—work pressures, family responsibilities—threaten to overwhelm us. Some of us get a headache or a cold. Others develop insomnia or become depressed or turn to drink. And in some people this physiological weak link is the back, so under stress they may develop a backache. This does not mean that the backache is not real, nor that it is entirely due to psychological factors; it just means that psychological factors may be involved to a greater or lesser extent in precipitating a given back pain at a given time.

People with long-standing back disease often notice that emotional stress will trigger a backache. One suburban mother who has suffered from recurring low back pain for many years says she "could feel the whole area tense up" when she drove in the driveway one busy afternoon, with houseguests expected momentarily, and saw that her teenaged son had not cleaned up the yard as he had promised. Conversely, recurring backaches can also take their own toll of the psyche. Another woman trained as a nurse and savvy about sickness suffered from a herniated lumbar disc for years before needing surgery. "Chronic pain," she points out, "is something very hard to deal with over a long period of time; it changes your personality."

Physicians sometimes see patients in whom they believe the psychological components of a back problem have become greater than the underlying physical problem. "I have a patient," explains one doctor, "a middle-aged man whose x-rays show only the degenerative changes typical of any person his age. These are normal x-rays. Yet he has gotten it in his head that he has 'arthritis' and he will not be dissuaded from it. He considers himself disabled from his job, which requires some lifting, and is now severely depressed. He is not a back cripple; he is a psychological cripple with back trouble." And occasionally physicians believe they see people whose back pains originate in the mind rather than the body. Because of the complexities of these mind-body interrelationships, physicians sometimes refer people with backaches, particularly those with long-standing back pain for which no physical cause can be found, for psychological testing or psychiatric consultation.

4

WHAT DOCTORS CAN DO ABOUT YOUR BACK

Sometimes it is obvious when you should consult a physician about a back problem. You or someone close to you may have had an accident and you suspect a broken back or other serious injury. Or you may have back pain or stiffness so severe that you cannot continue your normal activities. Or, rarely, a person will spontaneously develop paraplegia, as was happening to William Rubin because a tumor was squeezing his spinal cord. And in the box on page 84 we described how to inspect children for possible signs of scoliosis and kyphosis that should be discussed with your family doctor.

At other times, however, it is more difficult to know whether you need to see a doctor. The following are some specific danger signs or symptoms of possible back disease that should prompt you to consult a physician:

• *A backache that persists for more than two weeks.* Most backaches, like colds, go away by themselves in a few days or weeks. If a backache lasts longer, it may mean that it is caused by some more serious back disease that should be treated.

• *Pain that shoots down your leg toward your foot, or down your arm toward your hand,* whether accompanied by a backache or not. Such pain may mean that a herniated disc or other diseased tissue is pressing against a nerve in your back or neck.

• *Numbness in your leg or foot, or in your arm or hand.* This may mean that something is compressing a nerve carrying sensations from the affected limb back toward your brain.

• *Muscular weakness in your leg or foot, or in your arm or hand.* This can mean that something is pressing upon a nerve carrying messages from your brain to that limb.

• *A backache so severe that it wakes you in the night.* Most backaches feel better when you lie down. One that does not might be caused by some more serious disease, such as an infection or tumor, that should be treated without delay.

• *Inability to control urination or defecation.* Again, this is a sign that some diseased tissue may be compressing crucial nerves in your back.

• *Neck pain or back pain in a child.* While most adults, particularly as they get older, do have backaches from time to time, back pain is much less common in children, and is more likely to be caused by a specific disease that should be treated.

Whom to See about Your Back

Most people probably first consult the family doctor. There are several types of *medical doctors (M.D.s)* who are likely to serve as physicians of first contact. While the number of *general practitioners (G.P.s)* in the United States is diminishing, new specialists called *family physicians (F.P.s)* have been trained to take care of all family members, whatever their age, and also to treat many kinds of disease. As a formal medical specialty, family practice dates back only to 1969; today it includes about 25,000 practitioners and is growing rapidly. *Internists* (who number about 69,000) usually take care of adults from adolescence on, and specialize in internal medicine. They primarily treat disorders of the internal organs (such as the heart, kidneys and gastrointestinal tract) and also such diseases as arthritis and cancer. *Pediatricians* treat newborns through adolescents for all sorts of diseases.

M.D.s generally receive at least nine years of education and training after high school before they can take qualifying examinations and become licensed to practice: four years of college, four years at a medical school, and a year's internship (or the equivalent) in an approved hospital. Family physicians, internists and pediatricians all also receive an additional two years of residency training in a hospital before they can take further exams and become certified in their specialty.

Depending upon the particulars of your back problem, these primary-care physicians may or may not refer you to another specialist. *Rheumatologists* are internists who have taken two years of additional training to specialize in treating the many forms of arthritis. Orthopedists or *orthopedic surgeons,* who receive a total of five years training after medical school, specialize in treating people with injuries and diseases of the musculoskeletal system: the bones, joints and related nerves, ligaments and muscles. *Neurosurgeons,* who also receive five years of postdoctoral training, specialize in surgery involving the brain, spinal cord and other nerves. *Physiatrists* specialize in physical medicine, the use of physical agents such as heat, sound, electricity and exercise to rehabilitate disabled and handicapped people.

Many people alternatively consult *doctors of osteopathy (D.O.s)* about back problems. Osteopathy was founded in 1874 by Dr. Andrew Taylor Still, a Kansas frontier physician who had served in the Civil War. Dr. Still's original philosophy emphasized the central role of the musculoskeletal system in health and disease and the use of spinal manipulation—forcefully bending, twisting and stretching the spine—as therapy. Today, osteopathy has evolved into a parallel system of medical care utilizing all conventional methods of diagnosis and treatment (including drugs and surgery) while retaining an emphasis on the musculoskeletal system and spinal manipulation. Osteopathic physicians receive a scientific education and training generally similar to that of M.D.s: usually four years of college, four years at an osteopathic college, and at least a year's internship training in an osteopathic or other approved hospital before they can be licensed. Osteopathic physicians can also, like M.D.s, take additional residency training and become certified as specialists in fields like rheumatology and orthopedic surgery. In contrast to M.D.s, however, most D.O.s are not specialists: 90 percent are in general, family practice. There are far fewer osteopathic physicians than M.D.s in the United States (about 20,000 D.O.s, compared with more than 450,000 M.D.s), but their numbers are growing. Nearly two-thirds of them are concentrated in only seven states (Michigan and Pennsylvania have the most), and half of them practice in rural areas or in small cities and towns.

Many people also consult *doctors of chiropractic (D.C.s)* for back problems. Chiropractic was founded in 1895 by Daniel David Palmer of Iowa, who claimed that he had cured a man of deafness by manipulating his spine. Today chiropractic has evolved into a field of health care licensed by all states and recognized by federal government agencies (chiropractors can receive Medicare reimbursements). Chiropractors, however, are more limited than medical doctors and osteopathic physicians both in their schooling and in what they do. Chiropractors usually receive six years of education after high school: two years of college plus four years at a chiropractic college, with the fourth year including an internship in the college's outpatient clinics. Chiropractors do not employ as wide a range of diagnostic methods as do M.D.s and D.O.s nor do they prescribe drugs or perform surgery. Their primary method of treatment is spinal manipulation. There are approximately 23,000 chiropractors in the United States.

What to Tell Your Doctor

Some of the clues most useful to your physician in tracking down the cause of your backache come from what only you know about its history and its patterns. Be prepared to give your doctor the following information:

• What is the quality of your pain? Is it sharp? dull? knifelike? throbbing? intense? burning?

• How long—how many days? weeks? months?—have you had this spell of backache?

• Did the pain come on gradually or suddenly? If it started suddenly, what were you doing when it began? Did it follow an injury or any other unaccustomed activity?

• Exactly where is the pain? What region of the spine? neck? chest? low back? Does it extend to any other part of your body?

hips? buttocks? Does it radiate down your arm toward your hand, or down your leg toward your foot? (Pain shooting down the back of the thigh, following the course of the sciatic nerve, is called sciatica and is often caused by a protruding intervertebral disc.)

• Is the pain constant, or does it come and go in the course of the day?

• If it comes and goes, what is its daily pattern? Is it better or worse in the morning? late in the day? Does it wake you at night? As mentioned earlier, a backache that wakes you in the night is more likely to be caused by some serious disease, such as a tumor or an infection, that should be treated promptly.

• Does your backache feel better or worse when you lie down? Lying down relieves most backaches. If it makes yours worse, this is an important clue. What is the most comfortable position for you in bed?

• What else makes your backache feel worse? coughing? sneezing? straining on the toilet? bending or lifting? exercise generally? standing? sitting? walking? Most backaches are not aggravated by walking. If yours is, this is an important lead.

• What else makes your backache feel better? exercise or activity?

• Have you had previous spells of back pain? How often? How long have they usually lasted? hours? days? weeks?

• Do you have any other symptoms? Stiffness? What is its pattern? Is it better or worse when you get up in the morning? What makes it feel better? exercise or another activity? How long does it usually last? Do you have any numb areas on your body? If so, where? Are you aware of any muscular weakness in your arms or legs? Do you have any trouble with urination or defecation?

How Doctors Diagnose Back Diseases

Among the many diagnostic tests that a physician hunting the cause of a backache is likely to perform—or ask you to perform—are some deceptively simple maneuvers that nonetheless furnish important information. Your doctor may ask you to stand up, sit down, walk across the room and back, walk on your toes, walk on your heels, and bend your spine through its four basic motions: forward, backward, sideways, and twisting. When Paula Harris recently saw her physician for her "worst spell yet" of back pain, he suspected simply by watching her bend forward what was wrong with her back. "She was listing to the left. That was a good indication that there was a nerve root trying to slip around a bulging disc."

When Bob Alvarez, who subsequently underwent surgery for a herniated disc, was first examined by his doctor, the fact that Mr. Alvarez could not perform some of the tests at all gave the doctor a pretty good idea of *where* in the spine the trouble was. Mr. Alvarez could not walk on the heel of his left foot because he could not lift up the toes of that foot. When he walked, his left foot flopped on the floor, a condition doctors call foot drop. And when the doctor asked him to pull up with that foot against the pressure of the doctor's hand, Mr. Alvarez could not do it. All these things told the doctor that the muscle running down the front of the left lower leg (the anterior tibial muscle) was paralyzed. And this fact told him that something (the herniated disc, as it turned out) was pressing on the root of the nerve supplying that muscle, which was the nerve root leaving Mr. Alvarez's spinal column between his lowermost lumbar vertebra and his sacrum. On the other hand, if Mr. Alvarez had not been able to walk on his *toes,* it would have meant that muscles running down the *back* of the lower leg (the gastrocnemius and soleus muscles) were paralyzed and that something was pressing on a nerve root lower down, one leaving the spine through the upper part of the sacrum.

Some very simple tools can also uncover other significant clues. A plumb line can help assess scoliosis. Your doctor may use an ordinary tape measure to measure the circumference of your thighs and calves; if one is markedly smaller than the other, the muscle may be atrophied from disuse, another sign of possible pressure upon a nerve root. He or she may also measure your chest expansion (the difference between the circumference of your chest when you have taken a deep breath and when you have exhaled completely). If your chest expansion is less than two inches, this points toward a diagnosis of ankylosing spondylitis. Your physician may also use a small rubber hammer to test your reflexes, tapping lightly just below your knees and on the heelcords just above your ankles. This, too, tests the functioning of particular nerves serving muscles. If your leg does not jerk forward when the doctor taps your knee, something may be pressing on a nerve root leaving the spine between your two lowermost lumbar vertebrae. If your foot does not jerk upward when your ankle is tapped, something may be pressing against a nerve root lower down, one leaving the spine through the upper part of the sacrum.

If you have numb areas, your doctor may lightly touch various places on your skin with a feather or cotton swab or pin, asking you to close your eyes or look away and tell whether you can feel the touch. This is a very sensitive way of testing your sensory nerves. The specific pattern of numbness tells a physician which sensory nerves are being compressed. If you are numb on the *outside* of your foot, for instance, it indicates that a sensory nerve root entering the spine through the upper sacrum is being compressed, while if you are numb on the *inside* of the foot, it indicates that a sensory nerve higher up, between the lowermost lumbar vertebra and the sacrum, is being compressed.

Your doctor may also, with you lying or sitting on the examining table, move your arms or legs himself, bending your knees and other joints, testing both their strength and their range of motion. One of the most revealing of this series of tests is the straight-leg-raising test. While you are on your back, the physician will raise each of your legs in turn while keeping your knees straight and will ask you whether the maneuver causes you pain at any point. This straight-leg-raising test stretches and increases the tension on the sciatic nerve, which runs down the back of the thigh. If you have a healthy back, you may be able to raise your legs to 90 degrees without it hurting, but in a person with sciatica, this test will cause pain at a much lower point. When Paula Harris' doctor examined her during her spell of back pain, he found that he could raise her right leg to only about 60 degrees before it hurt.

The many diagnostic tests that physicians perform often assess a particular thing—the functioning of a nerve or a muscle, for example—in many different ways. This duplication of evidence usually enables doctors to detect malingerers, people who for one reason or another pretend to have a back pain they do not actually have. Such people usually perform inconsistently on the test. They will cry "Ouch!" to one test, yet will say nothing to another test checking the same thing in a different way.

Depending upon what your doctor finds in the initial tests, he or she may have you undergo a series of *x-rays*. X-rays, which show bone well, can readily reveal the details of the vertebrae that form the spine. Only after the discovery of x-rays near the end of the nineteenth century were doctors able to learn much about what could go wrong with the back. Today, x-rays are indispensable in diagnosing most back diseases. They can clearly show the narrowed disc spaces and osteophytes due to degenerative arthritis, the bone loss and crushed vertebrae caused by osteoporosis, and the slow slippage of the lowermost lumbar vertebra down the slope of the sacrum due to spondylolisthesis. In scoliosis, physicians measure on x-rays the degree of curvature. These data help determine whether the person needs to wear a brace or requires major surgery or simply needs to be watched. In ankylosing spondylitis, x-rays can reveal the characteristic appearance of the disease. Doctors sometimes call this bamboo spine because the calcified discs resemble the bulges on a bamboo stalk. (In the early stages of the disease, however, this look is not always present.)

Ordinary x-rays do not reveal everything. Soft tissue does not show up clearly on x-rays. If your physician suspects, on the basis of other tests, that you have a ruptured disc severe enough to require surgery, or if he or she needs to get a better look at other soft tissue, he or she may have you undergo myelography, a special form of x-ray developed in the 1940s. Making a *myelogram* is a more complex procedure than taking a conventional x-ray, and the person is usually hospitalized overnight following the test. First, using a local anesthetic, a physician injects a substance opaque to x-rays into the spinal canal, monitoring the injection with x-rays. Then the person, who is lying on a special tilting table, is tipped this way and that, to allow the substance to flow into all the nooks and crannies of interest, while x-ray photographs are taken. Myelography is one diagnostic procedure that can be uncomfortable, even painful, but it isn't necessarily so. After the procedure is completed, the person must lie flat on his or her back for some hours to prevent headaches.

Sometimes, in searching for the cause of a back problem, a physician will have a person undergo still other types of diagnostic procedures. When Charlie Hobbs had his mysterious backache and high fever, his doctor had him undergo a *bone scan*. To make the bone scan, a radioisotope called technetium was first injected into Charlie's bloodstream. Technetium is so similar to calcium, which the body uses to make bone, that it is quickly taken up any place new bone is being formed, which is also where bone is being destroyed by disease. Then a technician scanned Charlie's body with radiation counters, a completely painless process. "They ran the scanner close to me, really slowly over me, and it was just a matter of lying there." The resulting picture showed a hot spot in Charlie's chest, which could have been caused by a number of different diseases. Subsequent tests showed that his hot spot was caused by an infection.

Sometimes a doctor will recommend *discography*, another special form of x-ray. In this procedure, a physician injects a substance opaque to x-rays directly into an intervertebral disc. X-ray photographs are then taken to determine if the disc is diseased. This procedure is more painful than myelography, and the pattern of pain produced also aids in the diagnosis. Or sometimes a patient will need to undergo *electromyography (EMG),* which tests the functioning of muscles. A physician inserts needle electrodes into the muscles being studied, and then asks the patient to contract and relax these muscles. The electrical current generated by the muscular contractions is recorded and gives information about the health of the nerves supplying the muscles. Specifically, EMG can help determine which spinal nerve roots may be compressed by a herniated disc or other diseased tissue.

Occasionally a person with an elusive back problem will need to undergo a sophisticated new diagnostic technique called computerized axial tomography, usually abbreviated as a *CAT scan*. First introduced in the early 1970s, the CAT scan has been hailed as the greatest advance in radiological diagnosis since the discovery of x-rays in 1895, and its inventors, Allan M. Cormack, a physicist at Tufts University in Boston, and Godfrey N. Hounsfield, a British engineer, won the 1979 Nobel Prize in physiology and medicine for its development. A CAT scanner uses x-rays in a way that enables it to see much greater detail of soft tissues. A moving x-ray beam arcs around a person, making multiple exposures of a slice through the body, a process painless for the person undergoing it. A computer sorts out these multiple images and constructs a picture showing a horizontal cross section of the person's body that clearly delineates the internal organs and other soft tissues, as well as the bones. While CAT scan machines are enormously expensive (costing $500,000 or more), they have already become indispensable for diagnosing many diseases of the brain as well as of the internal organs, and will probably become increasingly useful in diagnosing some back diseases. When William Rubin found himself rapidly becoming paraplegic, a CAT scan helped physicians discover that his spinal cord was being squeezed by a rare but benign spinal tumor, which subsequently was removed surgically.

How Doctors Treat Back Diseases

In Chapter 3 we discussed treatments specific for particular back diseases, such as surgery for a herniated disc, estrogen therapy for osteoporosis, and bracing for scoliosis. Here we shall discuss treatments widely used for many different back diseases.

The advent in the mid-twentieth century of the antibiotic drugs, which can almost miraculously overcome many infectious diseases, seems to have given many people the idea that doctors can cure every disease overnight. This is emphatically not true for most back diseases. As mentioned earlier, most are chronic diseases: few can be cured, in the sense of permanent eradication of the underlying cause of the disease. In addition, they tend to flare up from time to time, often without any obvious reason, and then go away again on their own. Yet these diseases can generally be kept under control by a combination of treatments your doctor may prescribe plus measures that you can take at home (see Chapter 5).

Once the cause of your back pain or other symptoms has been determined, your physician may recommend one or more, depending upon the circumstances, of the following common treatments.

BED REST

Lying down is such an instinctive reaction to backache that it must be an ancient remedy; probably even our prehistoric ancestors sometimes curled up on beds of skins in their caves to wait out a bout of pain. Today, prolonged rest in bed is one of the treatments doctors most often prescribe for many types of back problems. One can take weight off an injured arm by supporting it with a sling; one can take weight off a leg by means of a crutch; but the only way to relieve the back from the weight of the upper body is by lying down. Scientific research has actually measured this reduction in pressure on the spine due to lying down. According to the studies by Dr. Alf Nachemson cited earlier, when we lie on the side, the load on the lower spine drops to only 75 percent of what it is when we are standing. With the pressure reduced, a sick back not only feels better but can also better go about the process of healing itself: inflammation can subside, and a bulging disc may even retreat.

Such prescribed bed rest may last from a few days to many weeks, and its strictness can vary. Sometimes people are hospitalized; other times they can rest at home. Sometimes they are not allowed out of bed at all; other times they are permitted up to go to the bathroom or to bathe or to eat. When Paula Harris, the mother of four small children, was prescribed bed rest for her bulging disc, she spent only a few days in the hospital. She then spent the rest of the time at home, where at first she was not allowed out of bed at all. "I just lay there," she recalls. Bed rest at home may sound like a simple and relatively inexpensive treatment, but in order to get Mrs. Harris' usual work done, her husband had to take time off from his business, and they had to round up relatives to help take care of the children and run the household. After two weeks, however, Mrs. Harris' back improved enough to allow her to get up half an hour a day. "I would crawl out of bed to get meals on the table, but then I would suffer for it." Nor is bed rest easy psychologically. "Several times I got really depressed. Once was after several weeks when I saw my little girl go to someone else," and again after four or five weeks, when her back did not seem to be getting any better. However, eventually the treatment worked. After seven or eight weeks Mrs. Harris was finally able to get up for good and cautiously resume her normal life.

Bed rest of varying durations may also be prescribed for people with acute back pain from many other causes: degenerative arthritis, spinal stenosis, spondylolisthesis, injury, a compression fracture due to osteoporosis. However, bed rest is not innocuous: it causes the muscles to become weak and the bones to soften. Thus too much bed rest is not a good idea for older people with osteoporosis, once the acute pain of a fresh fracture has abated, because it hastens bone loss.

DRUGS

While there is no magic pill to cure most back diseases, there are several categories of drugs that your physician may recommend, usually in conjunction with other treatments, to accomplish particular results.

If a backache is caused by an infection, your physician may prescribe an *antibiotic* to kill the offending organism. If the pain is due to a tumor, he or she may recommend *chemotherapy* with a drug to destroy cancer cells.

To relieve a moderate backache, the doctor may suggest a nonprescription over-the-counter *painkiller,* such as aspirin or acetaminophen, or a prescription drug like propoxyphene. For a more severe backache, physicians may prescribe one of the stronger narcotic painkillers, such as codeine, morphine, methadone or meperidine. The danger in using these narcotic painkillers, however, is that they can be addictive. Paula Harris' physician has also given her a prescription for meperidine, but she tries not to take the pills. "You can get hooked on them," she explains, "and I have enough of a problem. I don't need that."

To reduce any swelling of tissues that may be contributing to the trouble, a doctor may recommend any one of several types of *anti-inflammatory drugs.* Aspirin is probably the drug most frequently used, at least to begin with. Aspirin is a potent, triple-action drug —in addition to relieving pain and reducing inflammation, it also brings down fevers. Aspirin is usually the first drug tried both for rheumatoid arthritis and also for degenerative arthritis. Like all drugs, however, aspirin can also have serious side effects, the most common being gastrointestinal bleeding and ringing in the ears. If a person has side effects from aspirin, or if the drug does not do the job for him or her, other anti-inflammatory drugs are available. There are steroid drugs as well, such as cortisone. Each of them, of course, has its own beneficial action on the body and its own side effects.

To relax tense, spastic muscles, physicians can prescribe one of the minor tranquilizers, such as one of the benzodiazepines, which are also *muscle relaxants* and *sedatives.* These drugs do not, however, selectively relax back muscles; they can only relax muscles generally and are thus sometimes called "people relaxants."

BRACES, CORSETS AND COLLARS

The use of orthopedic appliances is also an ancient treatment for back disease: the second century A.D. Greek physician Galen advocated strapping the chest to correct scoliosis. Today a vast array of devices is available for many different specific applications. Generally, such orthopedic appliances help support and also immobilize the spine, keeping people from moving it more than they should. There are collars for the neck, braces and corsets for the torso. These vary in length, in flexibility, in the materials they are made out of (usually combinations of cloth, leather, plastic or metal), and in the details of their construction. They are often named after a person or a city or some conspicuous feature of their design—for example, the Thomas collar, the Jewett brace, the Philadelphia collar, the Milwaukee brace, the chairback and four-poster braces.

A person might wear an orthopedic collar for a while after a whiplash or other injury to the neck, or during an episode of pain due to a degenerated disc in the neck. Mrs. Joan Marchi wore a soft collar for seven weeks while she was recovering from surgery to her neck to fuse vertebrae damaged by rheumatoid arthritis. People might also wear a body brace or corset following surgery to the lower back, and the wearing of a rigid brace throughout the growing years can prevent disfiguring scoliosis in a teenager.

Mrs. Jenny Crawford had to wear a brace during the daytime after she herniated a disc while horseback-riding. Mostly made of cloth, it had two stiff metal stays up the back and more than a dozen other more flexible stays, and was fastened in front with three straps. "It looked like the old-fashioned whalebone corset my aunt used to wear, but it did not go so far down at the bottom or so far up at the top," she recalls, "and it reminded me to stand and move properly." After three months, she found she could do without it except for playing tennis. If she did not wear it then, however, "I felt unstable. I felt like my back might go out the next time I reached for the ball." Then, after several years of wearing it for tennis, she was able to go without it completely. Mr. Oliver Ballard, on the other hand, now finds that he must wear his orthopedic corset "pretty much all the time," because of the severe degenerative arthritis that so weakened his spine that he had to retire early from his piano business. While the corset is not noticeable to another person, it does interfere with the fit of his wardrobe. "You really owe me a whole bunch of new clothes," he joshes the doctor who prescribed the device, "because now I can't wear my old ones."

TRACTION

The word "traction" comes from the Latin for pulling or drawing; in medicine, traction is the application of a pulling force to the body or a part of it to straighten and stretch joints and other tissues. As a treatment for back disease, traction dates back at least to the time of the fifth century B.C. Greek physician Hippocrates, who described a racklike apparatus, made out of wood and leather and padded with robes, for straightening a bent spine. Today, physicians use a variety of contrivances to apply traction to the neck alone or to the lower back alone or to the entire spine, for different purposes.

People may be put in traction following a fracture or other spinal injury, or before undergoing surgery for severe kyphosis or scoliosis, to straighten the spine as much as possible. Mrs. Joan Marchi was in cervical traction for several weeks in the hospital and some at home to stabilize her neck while it healed from surgery.

A person with a herniated disc is sometimes put into gravity lumbar traction for a half-hour or hour or so. The patient is fastened into a special tight padded vest attached by straps to the head of a tilting table or frame. When the table is tilted upward, the weight of the person's lower trunk and legs stretches out his or her lower spine.

A person for whom bed rest in the hospital has been prescribed for a herniated disc is sometimes also put into pelvic traction by means of a girdlelike device around the hips. This device is connected to straps running over pullies and attached to weights dangling over the foot of the bed. Such traction is not enough to actually pull the vertebrae farther apart, but the traction keeps the lower spine in a good position while the pain subsides and the herniation heals, and it also ensures that the person remains in bed. Traction also makes some people feel more comfortable. Mrs. Jenny

Crawford, who spent a week in pelvic traction after she herniated a disc, says, "It just felt very good having the pull on my back. It was a relief."

PHYSICAL THERAPY

Physical therapy is a term used for treatment with such physical agents as heat, electricity, light, and sound. For such treatments, a physician may refer a person to a physical therapist (also sometimes called a physiotherapist). Physical therapists are health professionals who receive from four to six years of education and training after high school, obtaining a bachelor's or higher degree, and who also must pass a state examination for licensure. There are over 20,000 such physical therapists in the United States. Physical therapists also work with disabled or handicapped people, helping them to make the most of their abilities.

Heat is one of the physical agents often used in physical therapy to help relax tense and spastic back muscles. Heat can be applied to the skin overlying the problem area with hot towels, hot-water bottles, electric heating pads, infrared lamps or paraffin baths. Or heat can be directed more deeply into the muscles by means of diathermy machines, which generate heat an inch or so down with an oscillating electric current, or by ultrasound devices, which use high-frequency sound waves to penetrate even deeper. Conversely, *cold* is sometimes useful. Usually applied by means of cold compresses or ice packs, it decreases pain and spasm by numbing the area somewhat.

In addition, physical therapists often employ *massage* of many different types to loosen tense muscles, and *hydrotherapy* (whirlpool baths, which both warm muscles and gently massage them). They frequently work with people on *exercises*, both passively moving stiff joints and also teaching people how to exercise their joints and muscles themselves. They also sometimes perform *manipulation*.

MANIPULATION

The word "manipulation" comes from the Latin word for hand, and in medicine means the use of the hands to examine or treat a person. In a broad sense, manipulation includes the manual setting of a broken bone or dislocated joint. Spinal manipulation, specifically, involves using the hands to bend, twist or stretch the joints of the spine. Several kinds of health professionals manipulate the spine to treat back pain. Chiropractors use spinal manipulation as their primary form of treatment. Osteopathic physicians emphasize manipulation but also employ all other generally accepted treatments. And both physical therapists and some M.D.s also perform spinal manipulation on occasion.

Spinal manipulation is one of the most controversial treatments for back pain. Many satisfied customers swear by it, claiming it can relieve acute attacks of backache almost immediately. Critics point out, however, that there is little scientific evidence to explain why it works, or indeed, whether it does work. In 1975 the National Institute of Neurological and Communicative Disorders and Stroke, in response to a U.S. Senate directive, convened a workshop of fifty-eight distinguished medical doctors, osteopathic physicians, chiropractors and other scientists to evaluate both the effectiveness and the scientific basis for manipulation. The resulting official conference report, entitled "The Research Status of Spinal Manipulative Therapy," states that "specific conclusions cannot be derived from the scientific literature for or against . . . the efficacy of spinal manipulative therapy." Nor, the report also states, can specific conclusions be derived for or against "the pathophysiological foundations from which it is derived."

There are some back diseases in which manipulation cannot help or could do actual harm. It cannot straighten true structural scoliosis, nor can it put back a vertebra that has slipped out of place due to spondylolisthesis. It could increase the pain if a person had a herniated disc, and in a person with osteoporosis, manipulation might even cause a vertebra to fracture.

ELECTRICAL STIMULATION

In the 1970s a portable, electronic device was developed that can help alleviate chronic back pain for some people. Called transcutaneous ("cutaneous" means skin) nerve stimulators, the device generally consists of a small battery-operated black box with several flat electrodes attached to it. The person using the device fastens the electrodes to his skin at specific spots indicated by his or her physician, where particular nerve fibers come near the body's surface. When an attack of pain occurs, the person presses a button that causes the device to generate a minute electrical current that stimulates those nerves. Most people describe the sensation as a not-unpleasant tingling. "I felt the vibration," explains Mrs. Jane Davis, who used the device for a while after her surgery for spinal stenosis. "I was supposed to use the device for an hour, then off for an hour. When I had it on, I did not feel the pain. It just overruled the pain." Other people may find that the pain-free period lasts long after they turn the device off. It is not fully understood why these electrical stimulators relieve pain. One theory is that they block pain signals from reaching the brain.

INJECTION

The drug treatments mentioned earlier are ones that generally act on the entire body. Sometimes physicians also inject drugs locally, directly into a spastic or painful problem spot in the back. The drugs injected are usually an anesthetic or a cortisone derivative or a combination of the two. They may inject these drugs into so-called trigger points (areas of special tenderness or pain) in the muscles or near the facet joints. The injection of chymopapain into a disc, a controversial treatment for a herniated disc, is discussed in Chapter 3. As of this date, the Food and Drug Administration has not approved chymopapain for general use in the United States.

BACK SCHOOLS

A trend in recent years has been for physicians to send some people with continuing back pain to so-called back schools for an education on the spine. The curriculum of a back school usually includes subject matter similar to that covered in this book—the basic anatomy of the back and how it works, along with what can go wrong, with particular emphasis on how we can take care of the back. The format might be a series of weekly lectures by such experts as physicians, psychologists and physical therapists, or it might be a program of slides shown to a selected group, or it might consist of classes small enough to permit the instructor to give pointers tailored to a person's individual problem. Some back schools even give examinations at the end of the course to test what the students have learned.

A study at the Automotive Division of AB Volvo in Göteborg, Sweden, conducted by physiotherapist Marianne Bergquist-Ullman and orthopedic surgeon Ulf Larsson, demonstrated how much a back-school education could help. Of 217 people with acute low back pain, 70 who attended a back-school program (consisting of four forty-five-minute classes over a period of two weeks) were able to return to work significantly sooner than those who had other therapy. The back-school graduates were away from work for an average of twenty and a half days, while the others were out an average of twenty-six and a half days.

SURGERY

Of the many people who suffer back pain from time to time, only a very few ever require back surgery. "Most people with backaches probably don't even come to see us," points out one orthopedic surgeon, "and of those who do, I operate on very few."

Some circumstances do require prompt surgery: for example, certain types of spinal tumors or herniated discs. More often, however, physicians first treat people with the conservative treatments we have been discussing—bed rest, drugs, braces, traction, physical therapy. Doctors will consider performing surgery only if these methods do not work after a period of time. There are many back conditions, however, that surgery often cannot help: for example, extensive degenerative arthritis or osteoporosis.

The most common type of back surgery is probably *diskectomy*, the removal of a herniated disc, an operation we discussed in Chapter 3. About 149,000 people underwent this procedure in the United States in one recent year. A diskectomy (sometimes called a laminectomy) usually involves spending three to fourteen days in the hospital. For example, Bob Alvarez was in the hospital twelve days altogether, seven of them after his operation, and his physician let him—since he does not work with his back—go back to work three and a half weeks after the surgery. (A person who does work with his back, however, might be kept off work for several months.) Two and a half months after surgery, Mr. Alvarez was able to cautiously resume athletics.

Spinal *fusion* is a much less common and more extensive surgical procedure. According to the National Center for Health Statistics,

53,000 men and women in the United States had spinal fusions in one recent year. In a spinal fusion, two or more vertebrae are welded together, so to speak, by bone grafts so that there is no longer any motion possible in the joint between these vertebrae. To accomplish this, the surgeon prepares the vertebrae to be fused by cutting away their outer layers. Then he packs against the vertebrae many small strips of the person's own bone, usually removed from a hipbone, sometimes through a second incision. As these bone strips heal in place over a period of months, they fuse into a solid, immovable bridge of bone.

Such fusions are generally done for instability in the spine and are sometimes performed at the same time as a diskectomy. Mrs. Joan Marchi needed to have a fusion in her neck because rheumatoid arthritis had so damaged her ligaments that the topmost vertebra was sliding off her second vertebra, threatening to kill her at any moment. Her surgeon stabilized the joint by fusing the top two vertebrae to her skull. In severe scoliosis, surgeons sometimes fuse as many as thirteen vertebrae to straighten the spinal curvature as much as possible, usually implanting a metal instrument (often a so-called Harrington rod) to hold the spine straight while the fusion heals. With such a long fusion, the person is left with that portion of the spine permanently stiff. And some people with severe spondylolisthesis may need a fusion to prevent further slippage or to relieve pain.

It takes longer to recover from a fusion than from the removal of a disc. It takes the grafted bone about six months to grow together with the vertebrae being fused, and during that time the person's spine must usually be immobilized in some manner. When Lloyd Eagleton had a fusion for spondylolisthesis, to fuse his slipping, lowermost lumbar vertebra to his sacrum, he spent ten days in the hospital. On the seventh day after surgery, he was fitted with a long body cast that he wore for three months. Then he wore a rigid corset for three months after that. Mr. Eagleton was off work for six months. (A person who does heavy physical labor for a living might have to stay off the job from eight to twelve months.) Now that it is over, however, he finds he can "do just about anything I want," and he is totally unaware that he cannot bend that lowermost spinal joint.

A less common type of spinal surgery is *osteotomy*. This word comes from the Greek words for bone and cutting, and means the cutting out and removal of a piece of bone. In the spine, osteotomy is occasionally done on a person so severely hunched over from ankylosing spondylitis that he or she cannot see ahead. The surgeon cuts across the fused spine, surgically fracturing it, and removes a wedge of bone in order to reduce the deformity.

All surgery, like all drugs, has its risks, and the need for surgery in any individual case must be carefully balanced against these risks. There is a risk of death in any surgery, due to heart or lung problems or the anesthesia itself, but this risk is generally extremely small. The risk of death from general anesthesia for all types of surgery, for instance, averages about 1 in 1,600. In the most common back operations—diskectomies and fusions—the risk of death is generally no different from that in most other surgery. In an osteotomy to reduce severe deformity from ankylosing spondylitis, however, the risk of death during surgery is quite high: about 10 percent. This is because the procedure must be done close to the spinal cord, and also because people who need this operation usually also have poor heart and lung function.

In most back surgery, the most common risk is infection, which occurs a small percentage of the time. The risk most feared, however, is paralysis. The risk of general permanent paralysis differs markedly depending on *where* in the spine the surgery is performed. In the most frequent operations—diskectomies and fusions in the lower spine—there is no risk whatever of general paralysis. This is because the spinal cord ends well above this part of the spine. As mentioned earlier, the spinal cord tapers off several inches above the waist. A person occasionally may have some residual paralysis of particular leg or bladder muscles after such surgery, but this is due to the condition that necessitated the surgery, not the surgery itself. In surgery in the cervical spine, however, there is indeed a risk of permanent general paralysis. Here the spinal column does contain the spinal cord. This risk is extremely small, less than 1 per 1,000.

Another type of risk to be considered are the odds that a given operation will succeed in achieving its purpose. In most diskectomies for herniated disc, there is about a 90 percent chance that the surgery will succeed in relieving the pain, but these odds can vary for an individual depending upon the certainty of the diagnosis, the length of time the person has had the condition, and other factors. In most spinal fusions, there is about an 85 percent chance that the operation will be successful the first time.

Against these risks of surgery, however, a person must balance the risk of *not* having the surgery. Is the condition life-threatening, for instance? Or is it itself causing progressive partial or general paralysis or any other serious problem? In most cases, situations that may require back surgery are not emergencies, so there should be plenty of time for a person to weigh—in consultation with his or her physician—all these factors, and even to get a second opinion from another doctor if desired.

PAIN CLINICS

The small percentage of people who have persistent, intractable back pain despite treatment may be referred to a so-called pain clinic. The concept of a pain clinic was pioneered in the 1960s by anesthesiologist John J. Bonica, M.D., at the University of Washington School of Medicine in Seattle. Today most major medical centers in the United States have them. At pain clinics, teams of many kinds of specialists—anesthesiologists, orthopedic surgeons, neurologists, neurosurgeons, physiatrists, psychiatrists, psychologists, social workers—are available to evaluate the problem and offer an array of less common treatments.

5

WHAT YOU CAN DO ABOUT YOUR BACK

While physicians have a sizable armamentarium of treatments to alleviate the symptoms of back disease, as we have discussed throughout Chapter 4, nevertheless many of the most effective measures for managing the problems arising from these largely chronic diseases are ones that only we ourselves can take. In this chapter we shall present and explain many practical ways each of us can minimize the strain on the back and help prevent backaches. The causes of back pain are so many and so varied, however, that oftentimes a measure that may help one person's back will not help another's. The criterion you should use in following any of the advice in this chapter is simply comfort. If a way of sitting or an exercise is uncomfortable for your back, it probably is not doing your back any good. If some activity causes you pain, try not to do it.

Overweight

One of the most important ways, physicians emphasize, to minimize the pressure on the back—for any of us, whether or not we have back trouble—is to keep our weight down. The added strain on the lower back of even a few extra pounds can be great, far greater than the actual number of extra pounds. Part of the reason for this is that extra weight so often concentrates in the abdominal region, forming a potbelly, as is the case with the man shown in the illustration. Such extra weight so far in front of the spine tends to pull the body over forwards. To counteract this tendency, the back muscles must increase their tension, thus increasing the pressure on the lower back.

The farther out in front this extra weight is—that is, the bigger the potbelly—the greater the increase in pressure, due to leverage, or what might be called the "seesaw effect." Children playing on a seesaw seem to know intuitively that the farther out from the pivot point a child sits, the more his or her weight counts. If a heavy child and a light child want to seesaw together, they balance the board by seating the heavier child close to the pivot point and the lighter child as far out as possible. In the rust diagram superimposed on the overweight man in the illustration opposite, the triangle below the line symbolizes the seesaw's pivot point. The larger triangle above the line symbolizes the heavier child, while the smaller triangle symbolizes the lighter child.

The fact that this seesaw effect causes a weight to exert more downward force the farther out it is from its pivot point is one you can experience for yourself right now using this book. First, hold the book in one hand close to your body; you could probably hold it that way indefinitely. Now extend the arm with the book out straight, parallel to the floor, away from your body. The book feels heavier, and you probably could not hold it in this position for very long.

Physicists describe this seesaw effect in more technical terms. The seesaw is a lever; the pivot point is the fulcrum. A weight exerts a greater downward force the farther out from the fulcrum it is because of greater leverage. They can also calculate that if a person had ten extra pounds of weight on his stomach, centered ten inches in front of his spine, and the back muscles exerted their force two inches to the rear of the spine, then these back muscles must exert a force of fifty pounds to counterbalance the ten-pound weight—increasing the pressure on the lower back by this fifty extra pounds.

One of the first measures that Paula Harris' physician suggested that she take, in her efforts to avoid back surgery, was "Lose weight!" As mentioned earlier, Mrs. Harris has suffered serious backaches on and off for nearly ten years, and recent tests showed

THE EFFECT OF OVERWEIGHT ON THE SPINE

she has a slight bulge on the rear of one of her lumbar discs. Her symptoms are not now severe enough to necessitate surgery, but her doctor has recommended that she do a number of things to reduce the pressure on her back and to strengthen the muscles supporting her spine. "I'm now trying to rearrange my lifestyle around my back," says Mrs. Harris. Throughout this chapter, we shall discuss these various measures she is taking to avoid disc surgery.

Mrs. Harris is a statuesque woman nearly six feet tall. When she married, she was "real thin," she recalls, weighing about a hundred and thirty pounds. With each of her four pregnancies, however, she found herself putting on weight until by the time of her recent "worst spell," she weighed nearly two hundred pounds. With her height, she carried such weight well, but her doctor told her she should weigh around a hundred and fifty pounds—which meant losing some fifty pounds, no easy task. However, with back surgery at stake, she has managed, over a period of two months, to lose nearly thirty pounds. And when she learned recently that her doctor had described her, on her medical chart, as "moderately obese," this fired up her resolve. "I'm going home and lose twenty more!" she exclaimed.

Surprisingly, it is not actually known whether such extra pressure on the spine—from excess weight or perhaps from a lifetime of heavy lifting—actually *causes* back disease in people with otherwise healthy backs. However, physicians believe that for people with recurring back pain, such extra pressure makes the back hurt more. "Losing weight won't cure your back," Paula Harris' physician told her, "but it will definitely help it."

The seesaw effect is also part of the reason so many women suffer backaches during pregnancy, particularly during the last few months, when the fetus is the heaviest and also protrudes out the farthest. An epidemiological study of herniated lumbar disc conducted by Jennifer L. Kelsey, Ph.D., of the Yale University School of Medicine found that the more children a woman had, the greater her risk of herniating a disc. The women who had herniated a disc had had an average of more than three live births, while the women without herniated discs had had an average of less than two live births. Physicians recommend that women of childbearing years in particular should exercise to strengthen their abdominal muscles between pregnancies in order to minimize backache during pregnancy.

Posture

Some physicians believe that bad posture is a major factor in back pain, while other physicians believe it is not. The one body position many physicians do believe contributes to backache—at least in people with some kinds of back disease—is that shown in the illustration on page 132. Ironically, it is one that many of us have been taught as a "good" posture. It is the posture of "attention": chest up, shoulders back, stomach flat, and—this is the part that may be bad for some backs—buttocks protruding so as to throw the lower back into an abnormally accentuated arch. This arched posture is also called *swayback,* or technically *lordosis,* a word that comes from the Greek for curving forward, or sometimes hyperlordosis (the Greek prefix *hyper* means excessive). Other postures that can also cause a swayback are slumping, so that the shoulders and the lower back sag, or bending backwards at the waist with the abdomen protruding. Overweight also often causes a person to stand with a swayback to counterbalance any extra weight in front.

In people with bulging discs such an excessively arched posture can well aggravate back pain. When diseased discs bulge, they almost always do so to the rear, and when we arch or bend the spine backwards, the discs also normally bulge backwards a small amount to permit the motion. Such a bulge may well press painfully upon a nerve or other tissue. Paula Harris does have a tendency toward swayback, she recognizes, and her physician has also warned her that in her attempt to avoid disc surgery she should also "keep her back at least in neutral position and not allow it to sag." Swayback may also aggravate back pain in people with degenerative arthritis or other disease in the facet joints at the rear of the spine by exerting extra pressure on these small secondary joints.

What, then, does constitute good posture? "In the past twenty years our ideas concerning correct posture have changed greatly," points out pediatrician George H. Lowrey, M.D., of the School of Medicine, University of California at Davis, in his book *Growth and Development of Children.* "The physical educators and hygienists were once dogmatic about it, and rigid standards were established. We have since become aware that no one posture can be termed the correct one. We now recognize that . . . posture depends on the age, the occupation, the physique and the health of the individual." Generally, a person with good posture stands easily, gracefully, as

BAD STANDING POSITION

shown in the illustration below, without exaggerating any of the spine's curves and with each of the body's major sections—head, trunk, legs—balanced on the one below so that gravity does not tend to pull them out of alignment.

GOOD STANDING POSITION

A simple way of testing your posture is demonstrated by the woman in the illustration below. First, stand against a door frame or a wall in your normal posture, touching the wall with both your upper back and your buttocks. Now, slip your hand into the space between the wall and the small of your back, as the woman in the illustration is doing, to check how much you are arching your back. Your hand should slip easily into this space, almost touching the wall and your back. If you find quite a bit of extra room between you

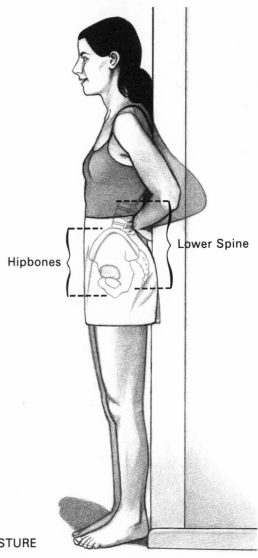

Hipbones

Lower Spine

HOW TO TEST YOUR POSTURE

and the wall, you may be arching your back excessively, and this may be contributing to backaches if you have them.

One exercise to correct such an excessively arched back starts from this position shown in the illustration on the opposite page. First, remove your hand from between your back and the wall. Now, step a few inches out from the wall, as shown by the woman in the illustration below, and try to flatten your back against the wall without bending at either your knees or your hips. To accomplish

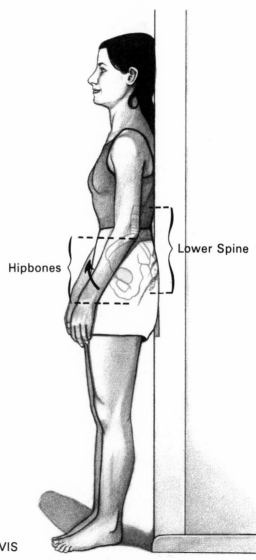

Hipbones

Lower Spine

HOW TO TILT YOUR PELVIS

this, as she is doing, you will find that you must tuck your tail under, so to speak, tilting your pelvis so that the lower part of your hipbones (shown in rust in the drawings) rolls away from the wall while the upper part of your hipbones rolls toward it—a motion indicated by the curved arrow in the illustration. Because the hipbones and the lower part of the spinal column are so tightly bound together, when we tilt the pelvis this way, the motion also inevitably flattens out the arch in the lower spine (also shown in rust in the drawings), as you can see if you compare the position of the spine in the illustrations on page 134 and on page 135. This exercise, called a *pelvic tilt,* also improves the flexibility of this part of the spine and helps make you aware of how much voluntary control you have over the position of this part of your back. We shall encounter this pelvic-tilt maneuver again in the section of this chapter on exercise, since it is part of some of the other exercises that physicians often prescribe to help people with back trouble.

The fact that an exaggerated arch in the spine aggravates back pain in some people is why wearing excessively high heels may increase backache in some women. High heels by themselves are unlikely to cause backache in a person with a healthy back, but they do force a person to change her posture somewhat to compensate for the altered position of the feet—just as you have to change your posture some to keep your balance if you are walking down a steep hill. And if you rebalance your body by leaning back at the waist and arching your back, rather than by bending backwards at the ankles, this could exacerbate backache. Mrs. Jenny Crawford, for instance, who has suffered recurring low back pain for many years, finds that she cannot comfortably stand in one place in the kitchen for any length of time in high-heeled shoes; they cause her back to ache enough to force her to slip out of them into shoes with lower heels. On the other hand, some men find that a medium-high heel *helps* the back. "I put my cowboy boots back on, with my heels, whenever my back hurts," says one midwestern dairy farmer who has undergone disc surgery. "I can tell right away it is helping my back. I don't know if it is that I am up on my toes a little bit more or what."

A position many people with back trouble find comfortable when they have to stand for any length of time is one saloonkeepers have long realized relaxed their customers: standing with one foot up on a bar rail, a low stool or a chair rung. Saloonkeepers do not necessarily have their patrons' backs in mind when they install a bar rail; they just know it relaxes customers, and relaxed customers are more likely to linger and to order another drink. There are, however, several anatomic reasons why this one-foot-up position is more comfortable for people with several types of back disease. When you stand this way, with knee and hip both bent, you also flatten out any excessive arch you may have in your spine, thus minimizing any ache due to this cause. Bending the hip also relaxes a muscle called the psoas; when the psoas is tight, it pulls on the lower back, increasing the pressure on the disc and also tending to arch the spine. And bending both knee and hip also tends to relieve sciatica by releasing any tension there may be on this nerve. Mrs. Crawford assumes this position, putting a foot up on a low stool, whenever she must stand at the kitchen sink for more than five minutes. "I don't always remember to do it," she says, "but if my back hurts, I remember in a hurry." Others use this position when standing at a workbench, behind a counter or at an ironing board. One orthopedic surgeon with back trouble always puts one foot up when he operates.

Sitting

We often speak of sitting down to take the load off our feet. Yet, surprisingly, scientific data show that sitting down (like being overweight) enormously increases the load on the lower spine. Experiments conducted by Alf L. Nachemson, M.D., of the University of Göteborg, demonstrate that when we sit with the back unsupported, the pressure on the lower discs is 40 percent higher than when we stand. For a person weighing 120 pounds, who has a pressure on the lower spine of about 70 pounds when he or she stands, the pressure jumps to nearly 100 pounds when he or she sits unsupported. For a person weighing 200 pounds, the pressure shoots up to nearly 170 pounds. The pressure increases so sharply, Dr. Nachemson explains, because when we sit, the center of weight of the upper body shifts forward (as it also does with a potbelly), and the back muscles must exert more tension to keep us from falling forward.

Many people with back problems notice this phenomenon for themselves. "Sitting really does bother me," says Mrs. Jane Davis, who had surgery for spinal stenosis. "I'm better off walking." People with bad backs often have trouble sitting long enough to enjoy a concert or a movie or to take a long airplane trip. Mrs. Marjorie Fellows, who has osteoporosis, finds that sitting at the bridge table "is torture sometimes." And after Bob Alvarez's disc surgery, his physician warned him that for a while he should sit only for meals, "because sitting puts so much stress on the lower back that it tends to retard recovery."

The fact that sitting is so hard on the back can even influence a person's choice of job. Sam Sutherland, for instance, is a tanned, athletic-looking young man, now in his late twenties, who has been supporting his family by working in a foundry. After an injury at work, he suffered a massive disc herniation that had to be removed surgically. Now, more than six months after the operation, Mr. Sutherland's back is still so stiff and painful that he is wondering whether he should go into some other lighter line of work. "People don't understand," he says. "A lot of people think that if you are injured and your back bothers you, they can sit you in a chair at a desk and you can do an office job. They think that if somebody has an office job, he isn't doing much. That work is pretty easy. And yet that's the hardest thing, that sitting, on somebody with back trouble. At least it is for me." And one woman with a bad back who used to work as a secretary would go home after a full day's sitting with a back so sore she would cry. Now she works in a greenhouse and finds this work much easier on her back.

Further evidence of the deleterious effect of sitting on the back comes from the epidemiological study conducted by Jennifer L. Kelsey, Ph.D., of Yale. In her analysis of over two hundred pairs of people with and without herniated lumbar discs, Dr. Kelsey found that people who sat half or more of the time on their jobs had a 60 to 70 percent greater risk of herniating a disc than those who sat less than that. And for people over thirty-five who had had their sedentary jobs for five years or more, the risk of herniating a disc was nearly two and a half times greater.

People whose backaches are aggravated by sitting devise many strategies to reduce the amount of time they sit. One executive tries to stand to talk on the phone and to confer with colleagues. A man who must drive on his job stops the car every thirty or forty miles

and gets out and walks around for five minutes or so. When M
Fellows plays bridge, "I usually get up and walk around when I'
dummy." And Peter Geist, who has undergone several back operations, finds that in church he cannot sit in the pew long enough for
the full service, "so I always sit in the big lounge in the back, where
we've got speakers and I can move around."

Chairs

Another important way of reducing the strain of sitting is to choose
a good chair and a good sitting position. All too often chairs are
designed more for their appearance than for their effect on the body.
Yet no single type of chair or sitting position is ideal for everyone
all of the time. We human beings come in such a variety of sizes and
shapes that a chair that fits one person perfectly may be all wrong
for the next. We also sit, during the course of a day, in many
different positions for different purposes; a chair good for desk work
may not be good at all for relaxing at the end of the day. And
furthermore, there are so many different kinds of back problems that
a chair or sitting position that is just right for one person's back may
be bad for another's. The main criterion in choosing a chair—
whether you have back trouble or not—is comfort, and probably the
best way of determining whether a chair is comfortable for you is
simply trial and error.

People who have long-standing back problems become very
canny, and understandably fussy, about their chairs and how they
sit. Some find they are most comfortable sitting bolt upright in a
straight chair. Mrs. Jane Davis has "a straight, up-and-down chair
at home that I can sit in." She has also gone through her house and
put "a board under everything, such as my davenport and my chair.
I even have a board on the seat in my car." Sam Sutherland, on the
other hand, says, "That straight sitting, I can't do at all!" Mr. Sutherland prefers a contour chair that reclines, so he can lean back and
put his feet and knees up. This position is very comfortable for many
people, with and without back trouble; it is the position we achieve
when we lean back in our office chair and put our feet up on the
desk. Mrs. Davis, however, finds that whenever she sits in this
position in a recliner, "It hurts like heck." Peter Geist has gone to

the trouble of "building sort of a wedge pillow for an old, uphol-
stered swivel chair. Then I put a cover on the chair with the pillow
wedged behind the cover. That's where I sit when I'm home. I'm
going to have to give it up one of these days though. It's going bad,
and my wife wants to throw it out."

Many people with back trouble even buy their automobiles primarily for the seats in them. "It is funny how individual it is," points
out one physician. "My wife and I each have a car with bucket seats.
The bucket seats in my car just happen to feel great for my back but
are totally uncomfortable for her. And the bucket seats in her car
are right for her and uncomfortable for me. If I ride in her car, I
have back trouble. If she rides in mine, she has back trouble."

Nevertheless, there are some general principles about chair design
that apply to all of us whether or not we have back trouble. It makes
sense to expend the most care in selecting the chairs we spend the
most time in, which for most of us are the office chair and the car
seat. The fact that people come in so many different sizes and shapes
means that office chairs that are going to be used by different people
over a period of time should be adjustable so that they can be altered
for each person's individual dimensions. And one must also consider
a chair's effect on other parts of the body as well as the spine. The
following are some of the most important features to keep in mind
when choosing office chairs and car seats:

• *Back support.* You can significantly reduce the great increase
in pressure on the spine caused by sitting unsupported by resting
the weight of the upper body against a back support, as the man in
the illustration opposite is doing. The back support should be high
enough to fit the back comfortably, and it is probably more comfortable for most people if it is slanted back slightly rather than straight
up and down. Some people prefer a back support shaped to support
the natural arch of their lower back, while others prefer sitting with
their tail slightly tucked under and their back flattened.

• *Armrest.* Leaning part of your weight on armrests also helps
reduce the extra load on your spine caused by sitting, as does leaning
your arms on a desk or dining table.

• *Seat height.* A chair seat that is too high, such as a bar stool from
which your feet dangle, is tiring because you must exert muscular

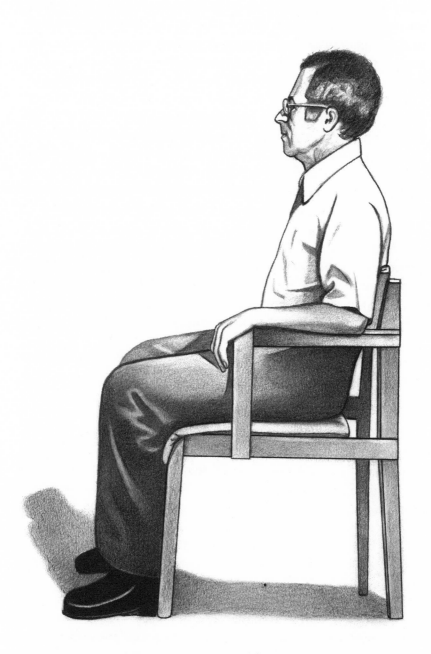

HOW TO CHOOSE YOUR CHAIR

o keep from sliding off of it. A too-high seat may also press nfortably against the nerves and blood vessels on the underside ne thighs. (Using a footstool or footrest helps overcome both se problems.) A chair seat that is too low, on the other hand, is hard to get out of for many older people as well as for people with back trouble. Very low car seats also often force a person to sit with the legs stretched out fairly straight in front, a position that people with sciatica may find uncomfortable because it tends to stretch the sciatic nerve. A chair seat is usually most comfortable when it is of such a height that you can rest your feet flat on the floor, as the man in the drawing is doing, with your knees bent about at a right angle so that your lower legs are perpendicular to the floor and your upper legs are parallel to it.

• *Seat depth.* A chair seat that is too deep for you forces you either to sit with your lower back rounded, a position many people find uncomfortable, or to sit forward in the chair without using the back support. A seat that is too shallow, on the other hand, may be tiring because it does not support the thighs sufficiently.

• *Overall size.* No one can sit in any one position indefinitely without shifting about. A chair is more comfortable if it is roomy enough to allow you to move about and change your position from time to time.

Bending

Simply bending forward—as we all do many times every day, when, for example, we lean over the sink to brush our teeth or rinse a dish, or we reach over the desk to retrieve a paper—puts even more strain on the spine than sitting with it unsupported. Dr. Nachemson's studies have shown that when a person who is standing bends the upper body forward 20 degrees, the pressure on the lower back increases 50 percent. For a 120-pound person, this motion increases the load on the lower back from 70 pounds to well over 100 pounds. This is for the same reason that a hefty potbelly and unsupported sitting increase the pressure on the spine. The forward shift of weight unbalances the body, and the erector spinae muscles must exert extra tension to counterbalance the tendency to fall forward.

A healthy back can bend this way without its doing any harm, but people with back trouble often notice that bending over with the legs straight—to weed the garden or pick vegetables, for example—makes the back sore. Surgeons sometimes advise people who have had back operations to avoid bending for a while. One of the many measures that Paula Harris is taking in an effort to avoid disc surgery is "to avoid leaning over as much as possible." One way to do this is to make sure that work surfaces are a comfortable height. Mrs. Harris has made a point of "just kind of rearranging things in the house so that everything is higher for me, so I don't have to do so much stooping." Another way to avoid bending is to squat down or even get down on all fours.

The combination of sitting unsupported *and* bending forward as little as 20 degrees—such as we do when, seated at a desk, we reach for the phone, or when at the dining table, we reach for a dish—strains the back even more than bending forward from a standing position. Dr. Nachemson has discovered that this common motion raises the pressure on the lower spine 85 percent, to 130 pounds for a 120-pound person. This source of back strain can be minimized by making sure that the desk or worktable is not too low in relation to the height of the chair. Draftsmen and architects often work at tables that can be adjusted for both height and slant. The rest of us should adjust our chairs not only for our own dimensions but also for the height of our desk.

Lifting

Lifting a heavy weight, like having a potbelly, puts an increased load on the lower spine far in excess of the actual weight involved, and for the same reason: because the extra weight is so far in front of the spine, the back muscles must exert extra tension to keep the body upright. This effect, too, has been measured by Dr. Nachemson. He has found that when we bend forward 20 degrees and also pick up a 44-pound weight, the pressure on the lower spine more than doubles, increasing 120 percent above the pressure when we stand. Thus, for a 120-pound person, lifting a 44-pound weight would increase the load on the lower discs from 70 to 154 pounds. And if we sit with the back unsupported and lift such a weight, the effect is compounded. The pressure increases 175 percent, to over 190 pounds for our 120-pound person. The combination of forward bending and lifting, and twisting, points out Dr. Nachemson, "really is the worst position of all, increasing the load by several hundred percent."

Yet it is not actually known, as we mentioned earlier, whether a lifetime of such heavy lifting causes back disease in people with otherwise healthy backs. The epidemiological study conducted by Dr. Jennifer L. Kelsey found no evidence of an increased risk of herniating a disc among men who did lifting on the job. But for people who already have bad backs, the increased strain on the spine due to lifting can significantly limit the ways in which he or she can earn a living. Mr. Oliver Ballard, for instance, who has severe degenerative arthritis of the spine, had to retire early, in his mid-fifties, from his piano business because his back would no longer permit him to help lift pianos. And Edward Reilly, a young apprentice electrician who herniated a disc at the age of twenty-four while hauling heavy copper wire, has been told by his physician that his back probably will not let him perform such heavy work for the many remaining years of his working life and that he should consider educating himself for some other less strenuous work. Mr. Reilly has had disc surgery yet he still has so much pain when he lifts that he "can hardly pick up my twenty-one-pound baby off of the floor."

Physicians often recommend that people who have undergone back surgery avoid lifting, as well as bending, for a time. One of the many measures Paula Harris is taking to avoid surgery is to cut down on the lifting she does. "I wasn't sensible about how I used to pick up things," she admits. "If I wanted to change the living-room furniture around, I'd pick a chair up and move it. And I used to pick up my boys. They are sixty or seventy pounds. If they fell asleep in my bed, I'd pick them up and take them over to theirs. Now I'm very careful. I don't move furniture. I don't pick up the children as much. I sit and have the kids come to my lap. I don't lift the baby any more than I have to. She's a little older now, so I just get her out of her crib, and say, 'Come on!' and she crawls out to the living room with me. My husband has rearranged the living room so that all the kids' toys are in one area. He brought in a little bookshelf, so all their storybooks and teaching clocks are all there. And when I feed the baby, I don't carry her out to the kitchen. I set her right there on the floor, on a plastic tablecloth, and she eats right where she is. If I took her out to the kitchen to eat, and put her in her high chair, and then carried her back into the bathroom to change her—that's two lifts that I shouldn't do."

We can do a lot to minimize the strain of lifting on the back by the way in which we lift. In the illustration below the man demonstrates how *not* to lift: he holds the weight far from his body, bending with his upper body nearly horizontal and with his knees straight, and tries to lift the weight with his erector spinae muscles. There are two reasons why this wrong way of lifting puts unneces-

HOW NOT TO LIFT

sary strain on the spine. First, the fact that he holds the weight so far away means that he must exert more effort to lift it from the ground than if he held it closer to his body, due to the seesaw or leverage effect we discussed earlier in this chapter. Second, the man is using his relatively less powerful back muscles rather than his more powerful leg muscles.

A better way to lift a heavy weight is shown in the illustration below. Here the man squats down and draws the weight close to his body, thus using his powerful leg muscles to lift the weight.

HOW TO LIFT PROPERLY

Sleeping

Many people with back trouble, and many older people generally, find it uncomfortable to sleep on their stomachs. "I can't sleep on my stomach at all," says Paula Harris. "All my life I've slept on my stomach part of the night," says Mr. Oliver Ballard. "Then about ten years ago I finally discovered that nevermore can I sleep on my stomach." "When I do sleep on my stomach," says another woman who has had recurring low back pain for about ten years, "I pay for it with a backache."

Lying face down, especially on a soft mattress, tends to increase the arch in the lower back, a position that, as we have discussed previously, aggravates backache in many people, particularly those with bulging discs or degenerative arthritis in the facet joints. Paula Harris notices that when she does lie on her stomach, it increases her tendency to swayback. "My back caves in completely and it seems to pop something out or put pressure on it."

As with sitting positions, however, no single sleeping position is comfortable for everyone with back problems. Mrs. Marjorie Fellows prefers sleeping on her side, while Oliver Ballard finds he "can only rarely sleep on my side. Usually I am on my back all the time." Paula Harris can sleep either on her back or on her side. Many people with back trouble, however, find it comfortable to sleep, whether they are on the side or the back, with both hips and knees bent. To do this, when lying on the back, you must put something —a pillow, a roll of blankets—under your knees to support them and keep your leg muscles from tiring. Oliver Ballard, lying on his back, says, "I can't sleep without pillows under my knees." This knees-and-hips-bent position is essentially a horizontal version of the one-foot-up-on-a-stool posture so many people with bad backs adopt when they must stand for a period of time. It flattens out any excess arch there may be in the back; it relaxes the psoas muscles that may be compressing the spine; and it also helps people with a tendency toward sciatica by releasing any tension on the sciatic nerve.

For people with healthy backs, however, an awkward recumbent—or any other—position is not likely to cause back problems. "A lot of people lie in bed or on the couch, head propped up on a pillow and neck bent, to read or watch television," points out one physician. "If they then complain about their neck or their back, it doesn't take very much to figure out that if the position hurts, it isn't good. But there are many other people who lie that way all the time and have no trouble at all. To tell them that they must not lie that way, that they are going to suffer some dreaded back trouble down the road, if they do that for a number of years —why, that's ridiculous!"

In one particular back disease, however, sleeping position *is* very important. People with ankylosing spondylitis should sleep with the spine straight so that as it fuses, over the years, it does so as straight as possible. Unfortunately, this may not necessarily be the most comfortable position. (This is one exception to the general rule that what feels good is probably good for the back, and what feels bad is probably not helping it.) Robert Van Dyck, for instance, who has ankylosing spondylitis, often has so much trouble sleeping lying down, because of pain in his back and neck, that he ends up dozing in a chair.

On the other hand, lying down, even briefly, helps many others cope with a bout of backache, and they often prescribe such therapy for themselves, a sort of mini-version of the bed rest physicians so frequently prescribe for people with back disease. (Bed rest frees the back from the body's weight and also flattens the lumbar curve.) "If my back starts to go out, if I start to get the pinch here," says Paula Harris, "I lie on the living room floor with a pillow: An hour will do it." For Oliver Ballard, it often does not take even that long. "It happened this morning," he explains. "I don't know what I did— I stooped over to pet the cat or something—but I knew immediately I was in trouble. So I just lay down on the floor and in about three minutes I could feel something in my back kind of shift gears, and I was all right."

Beds

People's choice of beds, if anything, is even more idiosyncratic than their choice of chairs. Some people with bad backs like water beds; at least one man sleeps in a hammock; and many people sleep in reclining chairs, with the head and upper body slightly elevated and the feet and knees up, or in hospital-type beds that can be folded to

achieve this position. Others, like Mrs. Jane Davis, sleep with a
board under the mattress. Peter Geist not only "got the hardest
mattress you can get" and put plywood under it, but also placed two
bricks under the whole structure so that the head end is elevated.
Still others simply sleep on the floor. Paula Harris' father, who also
has back trouble, finds that the only thing for him is to lie flat on
his back on a carpet-covered cement floor.

The one general principle about beds, for most people, is that
firmer beds usually feel better than softer ones. This is because a
mattress that is too soft allows the spine to sag into unnatural bends
that can be tiring to the muscles. Yet very hard beds are not for
everyone. "I had one doctor tell me, 'You need a hard mattress, just
like sleeping on a board,' " Oliver Ballard recalls. "So I got a hard
mattress, and it just killed me. I damn near died."

"When patients ask me, 'Should I put a board under the mattress?' " says one physician, "I tell them, 'First try the mattress on
the floor and see how it feels.' While a very hard bed may be good
for one patient, that same bed may be quite uncomfortable for
another."

Exercise

Another effective way each of us can help our backs—whether or
not we have back trouble—is to keep in good physical condition.
Physicians are astonished at the people they see with backaches due
simply to what might be called the tired back syndrome. "People
stay in fairly good physical condition throughout high school or
college, because of physical education classes," explains one physician, "but I see a number of women, particularly, who once they get
out of school don't really do the things they used to do. They don't
swim and they don't play basketball any more. They go directly
from school to motherhood. And you ask them to do a sit-up or raise
their legs up about ten inches, and they can't do even *one.* They are
absolutely flabby. You put them on exercises and get them to resume
some of the sports they used to do, and a few months later they are
like new people. And they haven't had to wear an orthopedic corset
or anything."

Swimming is one of the activities physicians most often recommend for people with back problems because it exercises many different muscles of the body while the water helps support the spinal column. "It feels good just to get in that water and feel kind of weightless," notes one young man who recently had disc surgery. One swimming stroke, however, that can aggravate backache is the breaststroke, which requires arching the spine sharply, a position, as we have discussed, that is uncomfortable for people with some kinds of back disease.

Walking is another good activity for most people with bad backs. Walking actually puts less stress on the lower spine than sitting without a backrest does. The Swedish experiments cited so often in this chapter have found that walking increases the pressure on the lower back a mere 15 percent, and many a person with back trouble notices, "I am better off walking than sitting."

Physical activity is particularly important for people with osteoporosis. Our bones need the pull and tug of the muscles working against them to remain in good health. People who are bedridden rapidly develop osteoporosis, and in space the astronauts—despite vigorous exercise—lose calcium from their bones so fast that scientists fear they may develop osteoporosis on long space flights. Mrs. Marjorie Fellows, who already has had one compression fracture of a vertebra due to osteoporosis, now also—on the advice of her physician—walks for exercise, with the hope that she can avoid fracturing another one. "It is the only exercise I can do," Mrs. Fellows notes sadly, "and it hurts lots of times when I start out. I was walking a mile the first part of this summer, but I just haven't been able to make that for a while. Yesterday I walked six blocks. And I don't do this all at once. I can do it by doing it several times each day."

For people with some other specific back diseases, physicians often prescribe individually tailored exercise programs. Teenagers wearing a body brace to correct scoliosis usually also do daily exercises to keep the spine flexible. And people with ankylosing spondylitis also may be advised to perform, every day, deep-breathing exercises and exercises to keep the spine as straight and flexible as possible.

For people with back problems generally, physicians commonly recommend exercises both to strengthen the muscles supporting the spinal column and to improve the flexibility of the lower spine, in particular. They generally caution, however, that people should not do any exercise that increases their pain. If an exercise hurts, don't do it. Among the exercises they most frequently suggest are the following types:

ABDOMINAL EXERCISES

The most important exercises for maintaining a healthy back are those that strengthen the stomach muscles. The spinal column cannot stand upright by itself, as was discussed at length in Chapter 1. Without the active support of the muscles, it would simply topple over. On the front of the spine, the job of supporting the backbone is done largely by the several layers of abdominal muscles. Doctors observe, however, that many of us have weak abdominal muscles, which allow the stomach to protrude and the back to sag. One of the many measures Paula Harris' physician suggested was to "Tone up your tummy muscles!"

To strengthen these key abdominal muscles, physicians usually recommend one or more exercises that are essentially variations, of different degrees of difficulty, on the common sit-up:

• One of the easiest is to lie on your back and then simply suck in your stomach muscles as hard as you can and hold for a count of five or so.
• Another easy variation is, again lying on your back, to raise your head far enough to look at your feet.

• A slightly more difficult version is demonstrated by the woman in the illustration. This is often called a half sit-up or a curl-up. To start, lie on your back with your arms at your side, in the position shown. (Some doctors recommend bending the knees, as shown here, while others prefer having the legs straight.) Then raise your head and upper back off the floor as far as you can without it hurting, as indicated below. This is an exercise Bob Alvarez's physician prescribed for him in the first few months after disc surgery, and Mr. Alvarez, an athletic man in his early thirties, found at first that "Even that gets a little strenuous."

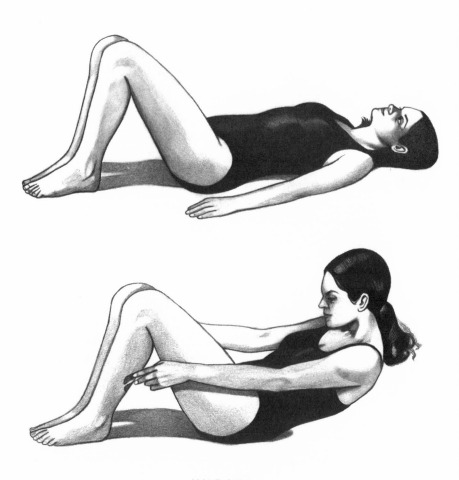

HALF SIT-UP

• Somewhat more difficult is the full sit-up demonstrated by the woman in the illustration. First, lie on your back in the same position as for the half sit-up. Then sit up, raising your entire trunk and upper body until your head reaches the level of your knees, as shown.

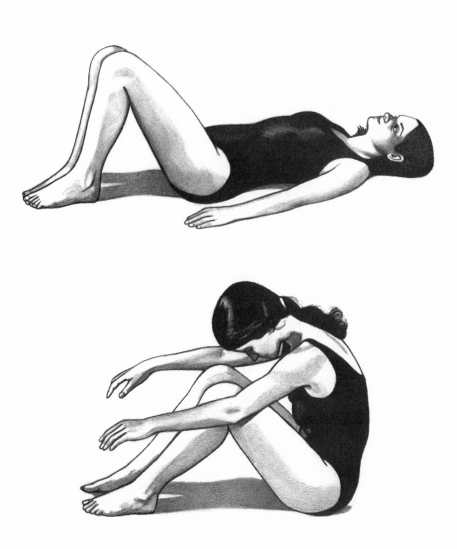

FULL SIT-UP

• Even more difficult is the sit-up demonstrated by the woman in the illustrations below. In this version, first lie on your back with your hands clasped behind your head. Then sit up until your elbows touch your knees. "I want my back patients," says one physician, "to work up to being able to do a minimum of twenty of these sit-ups."

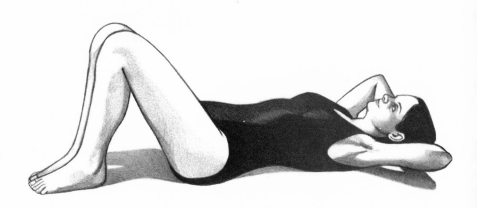

MORE DIFFICULT SIT-UP

There are still other abdominal exercises that doctors may recommend: doing a sit-up with your arms crossed over your chest; or doing one with your arms extended over your head; or lying on the floor and raising your feet off the ground. Occasionally physicians will warn particular patients against doing sit-ups in certain ways. For instance, if you perform a sit-up with your legs straight and your feet hooked under a piece of furniture, it strengthens your psoas muscles more than your abdominal muscles, and this tends to increase any swayback you may have, a posture that aggravates backache in some people. Or sometimes a doctor may tell a particular back patient not to do the more difficult sit-ups, since they do, Dr. Nachemson has also discovered, significantly increase the load on the lower spine.

ERECTOR SPINAE EXERCISES

Physicians less frequently recommend exercises to strengthen the erector spinae muscles that support the spinal column from the rear. This is because in many of us, these muscles on the backside of the spine are strong enough. The type of exercise that does strengthen these muscles is the following: First, lie on your stomach. Then arch your back so that you raise your head and shoulders and also your feet and thighs off the floor as far as possible. For an easier version of this exercise, keep your arms at your sides. For a more difficult version, extend your arms over your head and raise them off the floor, too.

This kind of exercise is often prescribed for people with ankylosing spondylitis because it counteracts the tendency of that disease to hunch the spine over forward. However, this exercise may increase back pain in people whose backaches are aggravated by arching the back.

PELVIC TILT EXERCISES

Among the exercises physicians frequently prescribe for back patients are other versions of the pelvic tilt. Again, there are several versions of these, of varying degrees of difficulty:

• One of the easiest is simply a horizontal version of the posture exercise demonstrated by the woman in the illustration on page 135. First, lie on your back. Then flatten your back against the floor.

• A slightly more strenuous version is demonstrated by the woman in the illustrations below. First, lie on your back, your arms at your side. Then raise one knee to your chest, pulling it down with your arms, as shown. Repeat with the other leg.

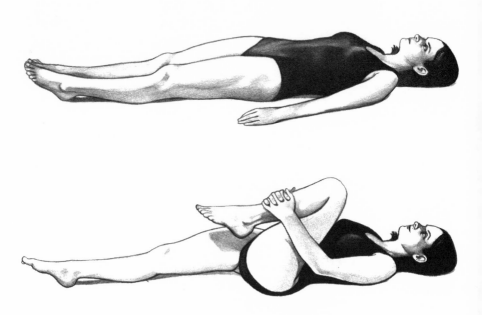

PELVIC TILT EXERCISE

• A more difficult version is demonstrated by the woman in the illustrations below. Again, lie on your back with your arms at your side. Then raise both knees to your chest, pulling them in with your arms, as shown.

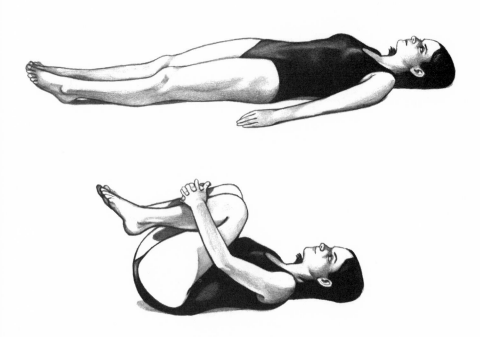

MORE DIFFICULT PELVIC TILT EXERCISE

These knee-to-chest exercises are so gentle that physicians often prescribe them for people too weak or in too much pain to do more strenuous exercises. These exercises do not strengthen the muscles supporting the spinal column, but they improve the flexibility of this lower portion of the spine and help make you aware of how much you can control its position. They also stretch the erector spinae muscles on the backside of the spine and help you overcome any tendency toward swayback by flattening the spine. And for people whose backaches are caused by backward bulging discs or degenerative arthritis in the facet joints, these exercises would tend to reduce such pain by opening up the disc spaces and joints at the rear.

OTHER EXERCISES

There are also many, many other kinds of exercises physicians may prescribe, depending upon a person's individual back problem and his or her strength. Sometimes they suggest exercises to strengthen the quadriceps muscles of the thigh (to make it easier to lift properly). Edward Reilly, who had disc surgery, was told by his physician to walk on his heels and toes. Another man, a dairy farmer, was told, after his disc surgery, to do knee bends. "I figured," he says, "why not do knee bends between two cows. I'll milk cows!"

There are three main themes, three types of advice, threaded through the many specific measures that Paula Harris is taking to stave off surgery and that the other people mentioned in this chapter are also taking to help their backs. First, avoid an excessive arch in the back; this advice helps many, but not all, people with back trouble. Second, minimize the pressure on the lower spine; while this may or may not prevent future backaches in people with healthy backs, it should minimize back pain in people who do have bad backs. Third, exercise to keep the abdominal muscles, which support the spinal column, in good condition. Perhaps the single most important message of this book is: some sort of sit-ups every day will help keep the back doctor away.

6

IS OUR UPRIGHT POSTURE TO BLAME?

It is often claimed, as we have mentioned earlier, that our unique, upright posture is to blame for the fact that human beings suffer so many backaches. To explore this question further, let us take a closer look at how the human back compares with those of other animals. What design features of the back do we share with our fellow creatures? What features of the back are different? And how did the structure of the back, over the hundreds of millions of years of its evolution, get to be the way it is today?

Whether or not an animal has a backbone supporting its body is such a fundamental characteristic that zoologists have used it to divide the animal kingdom into two major divisions: the inverte-brates and the vertebrates. The invertebrates are creatures *without* backbones. Some have completely soft bodies (worms, jellyfish); others have shells outside their bodies (snails, clams, oysters); and still others have stiff outer coverings (shrimp, lobsters, insects). The vertebrates, on the other hand, are creatures *with* backbones, whose bodies are supported from the inside by a rigid scaffolding or skele-ton. The vertebrates also have, as part of the back, a spinal cord. Upon this basic vertebrate plan, however, nature has devised many variations.

The vertebrates are relative latecomers to the earth, having been around for not much more than the last half billion years or so of the planet's four-and-a-half-billion-year history. The first step toward the evolution of the vertebrate back occurred about 600 million years ago, at a time when the present continents did not yet exist, and the land was completely bare. The oceans were teeming with plants and invertebrate animals whose shapes we know because they have been preserved as fossils within the rocks then being formed. In those primeval seas appeared a new creature, the ancestor of all vertebrates, whose precise shape we do not know because it had no hard parts to become fossilized, but who scientists believe resembled a modern animal called amphioxus. Only a few inches long, amphioxus inhabits shallow water in many parts of the world, spending its life largely buried in the sand and making its living straining food particles from the passing water. Amphioxus, however, has two design features that place it halfway between invertebrates and vertebrates. It has a cord of nerves running from its head to its tail, and its tiny translucent body is supported by a notochord, a somewhat stiff but also flexible rod of tissue, analogous to the notochord that is the first of the three "backbones" supporting the human embryo. Similar notochords also support the embryos of all vertebrates, and scientists thus believe that a notochord, in a creature much like amphioxus, was the first step in the evolution of the backbone.

From this animal evolved, over the next hundred million years or so, the first of the great groups of vertebrates, the fish. The earliest known fish were strange, ungainly creatures lacking the hinged jaws of later fish, but they introduced another design feature of the human back: the use of bone, a substance used only by the vertebrates and a stronger building material than those used by the invertebrates. These primitive fish used bone to make armorlike plates and scales covering the body. Since many fossils of this bony armor but none of any other bony skeletal parts remain, paleontologists deduce that these fish had skeletons and "backbones" made out of cartilage. Cartilage is the material forming the second of the three "backbones" supporting the body during its fetal months, and it forms the adult skeleton in some fish, notably the sharks.

The world's oldest known vertebrate fossils come from one of these armored fishes called *Anatolepis* who was only a few inches long and lived in warm tropical and subtropical waters, probably grubbing in the mud for its food. These oldest vertebrate fossils were identified in 1978 by John E. Repetski, Ph.D., a paleontologist with the U.S. Geological Survey. They were found in a pink limy siltstone from the northeastern corner of Wyoming. Dr. Repetski's discovery at one stroke pushed back the documented pedigree of vertebrates by some 40 million years: the siltstone was formed about 510 million years ago, while the oldest previously known vertebrate fossils were only 470 million years old.

The next step in the evolution of the back was the emergence, 400 million years ago, of more advanced fishes with backbones (as well as scales) made out of bone. These bony fishes, as they are called, introduced several new design features of the back that their direct descendants, the dominant kind of modern fish, still share with us today. The backbone is a column made up of many separate bones (the vertebrae) jointed together for greater flexibility than if it were a single bone. Each fish vertebra has the same basic pattern as the human vertebra: a vertebral body in front, a number of processes, and an opening that lines up with openings in other vertebrae to form a hollow tube protecting the spinal cord. Many fish, however, unlike humans, have ribs on every vertebra from the head to the base of the tail, as is also shown in the illustration, and they also use the back for a purpose we do not: propelling themselves through the water.

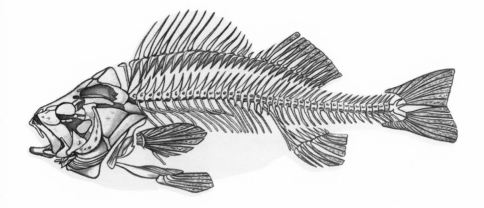

FISH

One of the most momentous events in the evolution of the back came about 350 million years ago when the second great group of vertebrates, the amphibians (the ancestors of modern frogs, toads and salamanders), first crawled out of the water. By then the land was covered with the first primitive forests (although there were no flowers yet), and the insects were just evolving. There was plenty for the amphibians to eat. With this change to life on land, vertebrate bodies also needed to change. Gills became lungs for breathing air. Fins became four legs for walking. With water no longer helping to support the body against gravity's pull, the backbone needed to become sturdier. While most fish spinal columns have only a single joint between each pair of ringlike vertebrae, the amphibian back-bone added another new design feature: additional joints between the vertebrae to interlock them, strengthening the spinal column and preventing it from twisting too much. These were the forerun-ners of the facet joints that buttress the human backbone from the rear. With life on land, vertebrates also evolved a neck, a feature missing in fish, useful for turning the head to look about. The amphibians never got very far with the neck, however. To this day, frogs and toads have only a single cervical vertebra, compared with our seven, and thus can only nod their head yes, rocking the skull on this one neck vertebra. They cannot shake the head no, because this motion requires a second neck vertebra to swivel the first one around.

The third great group of vertebrates, the reptiles (the ancestors of modern lizards, snakes and turtles), evolved from the amphibians about 300 million years ago. Their big contribution to human evolu-tion was not so much to the structure of the back as it was to reproduction. The amphibians have always been tied to the water because they must lay their eggs there. The reptiles introduced hard-shelled eggs, which could be laid on dry land, and this innova-tion freed them to conquer the land in a way the amphibians never could.

Dinosaurs stalked the earth some 230 to 65 million years ago (the Age of Reptiles). With backbones strengthened by interlocking vertebrae, some dinosaurs, the giant sauropods, became the largest land animals that ever have lived, with bodies sixty to eighty feet long, weighing fifty to eighty tons, and standing more than fifty feet high. Their vertebrae were enormous and were deeply hollowed out in order to attain size and strength without excessive weight. Among the dinosaurs' closest relatives living today is the crocodile.

Reptiles, like amphibians, have a sturdier spinal column than the fish, with secondary joints that interlock the vertebrae, as is shown in the illustration. One group of modern reptiles, the snakes, has the most vertebrae of any vertebrate. The anaconda, found in South America, has about five hundred. Snakes also, like the fish, have ribs on most of the vertebrae, from the head to the base of the tail.

REPTILE

From the reptiles evolved, about 170 million years ago, the fourth great group of vertebrates, the birds. The birds are an evolutionary offshoot with respect to the line that leads to human beings, and the new features they introduced to backs are ones that we do not share. The birds have elaborated the notion of the neck (initially developed by the amphibians) farther than any of the other vertebrates. Many modern birds have a neck so flexible they can twist around nearly 180 degrees, to snuggle the head between the wings in back, and they can also lower the head well below the level of the feet. They accomplish this versatility by having very long necks—swans have twenty-five cervical vertebrae, compared with our seven—and also by having neck vertebrae with joint surfaces specially shaped so that they can swivel about. Below the neck, however, birds have little flexibility, as shown in the illustration of the chicken on page 164. Birds have many of their thoracic vertebrae fused to help form a solid fuselage to support the wings. Behind this fuselage, most of the rest of the vertebrae (the remaining thoracic, lumbar, sacral and some tail vertebrae) are also fused into a single bone called a synsacrum to form a rigid framework for their type of two-footed walking.

BIRD

From the reptiles, there also evolved, about 200 million years ago, the mammals, the fifth of the great groups of vertebrate animals and the group to which we belong. The mammals began emerging well before the last days of the dinosaurs' reign, at a time before the continents reached their present shapes and positions, but when the land was finally covered with forests. Since the dinosaurs and so many other creatures suddenly and mysteriously died out about 65 million years ago, mammals have dominated the earth. These last 65 million years are thus called the Age of Mammals. Again, the major advances introduced by the mammals were not so much to the back as to other parts of the body. Mammals are usually covered with fur or hair instead of scales or feathers. We generally bear our young alive, rather than lay eggs, and we suckle our infants with milk secreted by the mammary glands. (The word "mammary" comes from the Latin word for breast, which is also the root of the word "mammal.") Above all, however, mammals are smarter than the other four groups of vertebrate animals. "In enterprise and ingenuity," pointed out zoologists Alfred Sherwood Romer, Ph.D., of Harvard University and Thomas S. Parson, Ph.D., of the University of Toronto in their book *The Vertebrate Body*, "even the stupidest of mammals is an intellectual giant compared with any reptile." Today the mammals encompass such diverse kinds of creatures as the carnivores (including cats and dogs), the hoofed animals (including horses and cows), the rodents (including squirrels, rats and mice)—the most numerous mammals—and the primates (including monkeys, apes and us).

Mammalian backs have some features in common, as shown in the illustration of a rabbit below. Curiously, while reptiles and birds both have variable numbers of cervical vertebrae, virtually all mammals, including us, have exactly seven vertebrae in the neck.

MAMMAL

(Among the exceptions are tree sloths and manatees.) Thus the giraffe, with its extraordinarily long neck, and the whale, with no visible neck at all, both have seven cervical vertebrae. While fish usually have ribs on every vertebra except the tail, and reptiles may or may not have ribs on most vertebrae, we mammals typically have a substantial section of the spine—the lumbar region—free from ribs or any other bony support. Here the muscles must help support the spine, and it is here that humans most often suffer backaches.

As we have now seen, our back is one of the most ancient structures of the body, older than our arms or legs, older yet than our way of reproducing. Many of its most fundamental design features —the division of the spinal column into separate vertebrae, the basic plan of a vertebra and its encirclement of the spinal cord—go back hundreds of millions of years to our fish ancestors. The interlocking secondary joints at the rear of our spine go back to the first land-living amphibians. The free lumbar area we share with fellow mammals.

Yet two of our back's most important design features humans share with no other animal. One is that as we walk with our characteristic two-footed stride, the spine is completely upright. A few other animals also walk on two feet. Some dinosaurs did; and today the birds do regularly, as do kangaroos, bears (occasionally), and, infrequently, our closest relatives among our fellow primates, the great apes—chimpanzees, gorillas and orangutans. But none of these animals has a completely upright spine or an easy stride like our own. Even the great apes walk most of the time on all fours, steadying themselves on their knuckles. When they do stand up, briefly, their posture and gait is very different from ours. They walk with knees and hips bent, and the upper body leaning forward.

The second important feature we share with no other animal is the curvature of our spinal column, the four curves shown in the illustration on page 22. This is very different from the curvature of the gorilla spine, which arcs in a single curve with no lumbar curve or arch at all.

The primates, ourselves included, differ from other mammals in, among many traits, our livelier intelligence and curiosity, our greater reliance on vision than on smell, and our versatile, grasping hands—useful for hanging on to trees and manipulating objects.

Many primates hold the spine erect more than other mammals do. Apes do sometimes walk upright, and monkeys often sit straight up or hold the trunk vertically as they swing through the trees. The human line must have evolved from some relatively primitive primate, some common ancestor of apes and humans. The fossil record, however, has too many gaps in it for us to trace the precise sequence of steps that led from a tree-swinging primate to a ground-striding human. When did the split between apes and humans take place? As long as 15 million or more years ago? As recently as 5 million years ago? What were the postures and gaits of these early ancestors? These are currently matters of lively scientific controversy.

We do know unequivocally, however—thanks to a remarkable series of discoveries in Africa during the 1970s—that our unique upright posture of the spine and our two-footed gait were fully evolved by nearly 4 million years ago. One of the discoveries was an extraordinary set of footprints found during the late 1970s by archaeologist Mary D. Leakey, wife of the late anthropologist Louis S. B. Leakey, at Laetoli in northern Tanzania. There are more than fifty footprints, forming a trail nearly eighty feet long, in rock that has been dated by the potassium-argon method to 3.6 to 3.8 million years ago. From these footprints can be read a poignant story. They were made at the beginning of a rainy season; it was sprinkling off and on. To the east, a volcano was puffing periodically, blanketing the plain with ash. Across this damp ash walked two creatures, perhaps together, perhaps separately, leaving impressions of their feet as clearly as any one of us might in damp cement. From the length of the creatures' feet, anthropologists have calculated that one was almost five feet, the other about four feet tall. Perhaps they were a male and a female. From the form of the prints, which are remarkably similar to what yours and mine would have been, anthropologists can tell that the creatures had a modern stride and walked fully erect. The footprints also show that the larger creature strode unhesitantly across the damp ash. The smaller creature, however, walked part of the way across and then—in a very humanlike gesture—paused a moment and turned toward the west, its back to the volcano, and then turned and walked on again.

Who made these eloquent footprints? One of the prime candidates is a proto-human creature called Australopithecus. This name, bestowed in the 1920s, means southern ape, but we now know that these creatures were neither southern nor apes. Many Australopithecus fossils have now been found. Among the most famous is Lucy, so named by her discoverer, Donald Johanson, Ph.D., director of the International Institute for the Study of Human Origins in Berkeley, California, who found her in the Afar region of Ethiopia in 1974. Lucy is one of the oldest (more than 3 million years) and the most complete (Dr. Johanson found 40 percent of her skeleton) of any of the known pre-humans. From the study of her and the many other Australopithecus fossils, anthropologists have a pretty good picture of what these creatures were like. They ranged from South Africa to Ethiopia, in East Africa, and flourished from at least 4 until almost 1 million years ago. Like the makers of the footprints at Laetoli, they were small. Lucy was only three feet six inches tall and weighed about sixty pounds. The largest was about five feet and maybe two hundred or more pounds. Their brains were the sizes of apes' brains—Lucy's head "was not much larger than a softball," says Dr. Johanson—and their faces were more apelike than human. Yet the fact that they were also humanlike is shown by the forms of their foot, leg, hip and other bones: they unquestionably —like the makers of the Laetoli footprints—walked fully upright with a stride as easy and graceful as yours and mine.

Exactly where on the human family tree the several different species of Australopithecus may or may not belong is also a matter of lively controversy, but the discoveries do make it very clear that the upright posture of our spinal column long preceded the expansion of the brain to its present size. The Laetoli footprints are more than a million years older than the earliest known stone tools (evidence of at least some incipient braininess), nearly 2 million years older than the earliest undisputed date for a fossil skull with a significantly bigger brain, and well over 3 million years older than our human species, *Homo sapiens.* At what point along the line the spinal column also developed its unique curvature is not known exactly, but the feature goes back at least 3 million years, and presumably to the beginning.

And what caused our ancestors to start holding the spinal column upright permanently? Some anthropologists believe it was in order to see farther over the African plains. Others suggest that it was in order to carry food back to a home base for the family. We may never know, but walking erect did free the hands for multifarious activities. Many scientists believe that the erect spine enabled an increased use of the hands that spurred the expansion of the brain. "Upright posture," says paleontologist Stephen Jay Gould, Ph.D., of Harvard University, "was the trigger of human evolution."

Is upright posture to blame for back problems today? As we have seen, human upright posture is no new evolutionary trait. We have had at least 4 million years of practice at it.

The question raises, of course, another question: whether other animals with horizontal spines have less back trouble than humans do. There is at least one specific back disease that human beings can have that no other animal is known to develop in quite the same way. This is the condition called spondylolisthesis, in which the entire upper part of the spinal column, impelled by the weight of the upper body, slides downward on the sloping surface of the sacrum. According to Leon L. Wiltse, M.D., an orthopedic surgeon who has made a special study of this disease, not even the great apes, human beings' closest relatives, develop this disease. The reason seems to lie in the differences between postures. While the apes do stand erect some of the time, they do not chronically have the weight of the upper body pressing down upon the lower spine as we do. This form of spondylolisthesis thus does seem to be part of our uniquely human heritage.

Some of the other back diseases affecting humans, however, do also afflict other animals. For example, herniated intervertebral discs are common in dogs, particularly in certain breeds, such as dachshunds, poodles and beagles, according to Eric J. Trotter, D.V.M., director of the Small Animal Clinic and chief of surgery, the New York State College of Veterinary Medicine at Cornell University. Dogs also are affected with a variety of spinal disorders similar to those in man, including degenerative arthritis, rheumatoid arthritis, ankylosing spondylitis, spinal stenosis, scoliosis and kyphosis, and spina bifida and other congenital defects. Cats are also subject to spinal disorders, although less commonly than dogs. Degenerative arthritis, one of the commonest causes of human backaches, also affects several other vertebrate groups: reptiles (it has been found on the bones of the giant dinosaurs), birds, and many other—but, curi-

ously, not all—mammals, including rabbits, horses and some primates. Yet whether or not these animals suffer backaches as much
as humans do is something that in the end we can never know. As
mentioned earlier, human beings not infrequently have backaches
for which no specific cause can be found, in which x-rays and other
diagnostic tests fail to reveal anything amiss. Thus, even if someone
went to the trouble of x-raying the spines of a lot of other animals,
we still would not know whether their backs hurt—for the simple
reason that they cannot tell us.

Even if we do have more backaches than other animals, there is
another important factor involved in addition to that of the upright
posture: longevity. Humans live relatively longer, past the repro-
ductive years, than do most other animals, and some of the most
common causes of back trouble are the changes that occur in the
spine as a part of aging. If other animals lived as long as humans do,
perhaps their backs would hurt too. Certainly anyone who has
watched an elderly dog limp around the house could not be sure that
the animal did *not* have a backache among his or her other obvious
aches and pains.

Whether or not the unique upright human posture causes backaches, it does help determine *where* the back hurts. As discussed in
Chapter 1, the region of the back that most often aches is the lower
spine, which due to the erect posture must carry more than half the
weight of the body. This is also the region of the spine that, as in
nearly all mammals, has no ribs to help support it but relies instead
on support from the muscles. The structure of the spine also helps
determine which of the discs are most likely to herniate and where
the spine is most likely to break.

Blaming human back problems on upright posture is not a very
productive thesis, since there is not too much we can do to change
human posture. We can hardly undo millions of years of evolution
and go back to scampering about on all fours.

GLOSSARY

A

ankylosing spondylitis
A form of arthritis in which the spine slowly fuses into a rigid rod. Also called stiff spine, frozen spine, poker spine, ankylosing spondyloarthrosis and Marie-Strümpell disease.

ankylosing spondyloarthrosis
See ankylosing spondylitis.

annulus fibrosus
Latin for fibrous ring. The outer portion of the intervertebral disc.

apophyseal joints
See facet joints.

arthritis
An inflammation of a joint. There are a hundred or more different types of arthritis, ranging in severity from slight to extremely serious.

atlas
The topmost vertebra in the neck.

axis
The second vertebra in the neck.

B
backbone
See spinal column.

C
cartilage
A type of body tissue that is slightly stiff but also flexible. Cartilage forms the second "backbone" in the developing embryo and also, in the child and adult, forms the nose and ears and the discs between the vertebrae.

cartilaginous

An adjective meaning made out of carti-lage.

CAT scan

CAT is short for computerized axial tomography. A CAT scanner produces three-dimensional x-ray pictures, which enable the physician to see greater detail of soft tissues.

cauda equina

Latin for horse's tail. The spinal cord tapers off several inches above the waist; below this, individual nerve fibers run downward through the spinal canal in parallel, vertical strands collectively called the cauda equina.

cervical

An adjective meaning pertaining to the neck.

cervical vertebrae

The seven neck vertebrae.

coccyx

The vestigial tailbone, the lowermost bone in the spine.

compression fracture

In the spine, a crushing down of a verte-bra, often due to osteoporosis, so that the vertebra loses some or most of its height and becomes wedge-shaped. Also called a crush fracture.

crush fracture

See compression fracture.

D

degenerative arthritis

The most common and least serious type of arthritis affecting the spine. In-tervertebral discs dry out and deflate; the vertebrae settle and also develop, around their rims, ridges of bone called osteophytes. Also called osteoarthritis, osteoarthrosis, wear-and-tear arthritis, old-age arthritis, degenerative joint dis-ease, degenerative disc disease, and spondylosis.

degenerative disc disease

See degenerative arthritis.

degenerative joint disease

See degenerative arthritis.

disc

See intervertebral disc.

disc joint

A primary, weight-bearing joint of the spine formed by an intervertebral disc connecting two adjacent vertebrae.

diskectomy

The surgical removal of a portion of an intervertebral disc.

displaced disc	*See* herniated disc.
F	
facet joints	Small paired secondary joints that buttress the spine from the rear and substantially stiffen it. Also called apophyseal joints or simply posterior joints.
foramen (*pl.* foramina)	A natural opening or passage, especially one into or through a bone.
frozen spine	*See* ankylosing spondylitis.
fusion	In the spine, a surgical procedure in which two or more vertebrae are permanently fused together by bone grafts.
H	
herniated disc	Blisterlike bulging or protrusion of the contents of the disc out through the annular fibers that normally hold them in place. Also called ruptured disc, slipped disc and displaced disc.
hunchback	*See* kyphosis.
I	
intervertebral disc	One of a number of cylindrical elastic pads, made of fibrocartilage, that both separate and join each pair of vertebrae in the spine.
K	
kyphosis	Abnormally accentuated curvature of the thoracic region of the spine. Also called hunchback or roundback.
L	
laminectomy	An operation in which the surgeon cuts through the lamina of a vertebra (the portion between the spinous and transverse processes). Often performed to reach a herniated disc in order to remove it.
ligament	A tough, elastic band of tissue that binds the bones together and reinforces the joints. In the spine, ligaments bind the vertebrae together and reinforce both the disc and the facet joints.
lordosis	An abnormally accentuated arch in the lower spine. Also called swayback.
lumbar	An adjective that means pertaining to the loins, the part of the body between the ribs and hipbones.

lumbar vertebrae

The five large vertebrae in the lower portion of the spine, between the ribs and the sacrum.

M

Marie-Strümpell disease

See ankylosing spondylitis.

meninx (*pl.* meninges)

Any of the three membranes enveloping the brain and spinal cord.

muscle

A type of body tissue that is able, upon command from nerves, to contract to move the skeleton and other body parts through space.

myelography

A special form of x-ray, in which a substance opaque to x-rays is injected into the spinal canal.

N

nerve

A filament of tissue that carries messages from the brain to the body or from the body back to the brain.

nerve roots

The portions of nerve bundles emerging from the spine between each successive pair of vertebrae.

nucleus pulposus

Latin for pulpy nucleus. The pulpy, jellylike central portion of the intervertebral disc. Often just called the nucleus.

O

old-age arthritis

See degenerative arthritis.

orthopedic

An adjective that means pertaining to orthopedics.

orthopedics

The medical specialty concerned with the treatment of injuries and diseases of the musculoskeletal system, including the bones, joints, ligaments, muscles and related nerves.

osteoarthritis

See degenerative arthritis.

osteoarthrosis

See degenerative arthritis.

osteophyte

A projecting outgrowth from a bone, often called a spur.

osteoporosis

Loss of bone substance and decrease of bone density. A condition that causes the bones to become softer, more porous and more likely to break.

osteotomy	The surgical cutting of bone.

P

pelvic tilt	An exercise in which a person tilts the pelvis so that the lower part rolls forward while the upper part rolls backward.
pelvis	Hip region; the lower part of the trunk of the body.
poker spine	*See* ankylosing spondylitis.
posterior joints	*See* facet joints.
psoas muscle	A muscle in the lumbar region of the spine. The psoas muscles primarily move the legs.

R

rheumatoid arthritis	One of the most painful and crippling types of arthritis. It is a body-wide disease that attacks and destroys joints, particularly those of the hands, wrists, elbows, feet, knees, hips and spine.
roundback	*See* kyphosis.
ruptured disc	*See* herniated disc.

S

sacroiliac joint	One of the joints connecting the sacrum with the hipbones.
sacrum	The largest bone in the spine; wedged firmly between the hipbones, it is formed during the growing years by the fusion of five individual vertebrae.
sciatic nerve	The largest nerve in the body. Formed in the hip region, one on either side, from several nerves that emerge from the lower part of the spine, the sciatic nerves run down the back of either thigh as far as the knee, where they branch into other nerves.
sciatica	Pain along the pathway of the sciatic nerve.
scoliosis	Abnormal sideways curvature of the spine. From the Greek word for crookedness.
spina bifida	An uncommon and catastrophic congenital defect of the spine in which a

vertebra has a large gap at the rear, through which some of the contents of the spinal canal may protrude. Also called spina bifida with meningomyelocele.

spina bifida occulta A common, usually not serious congenital defect of the spine in which a vertebra has a small gap at the rear. Also popularly called a "hole in the spine."

spinal canal The hollow vertical tunnel within the spinal column, formed by the vertebrae, that encloses and protects the spinal cord.

spinal column The column of vertebrae that supports the back and protects the spinal cord. Also called the spine, the backbone or the vertebral column.

spinal cord A delicate bundle of nerve fibers, about the diameter of the little finger, that runs vertically from the base of the brain down through the spinal canal within the spinal column.

spinal stenosis Any abnormal narrowing of the spinal canal or of an intervertebral foramen (the opening between the vertebrae at the side through which the nerve root emerges).

spine *See* spinal column.

spondylitis Any inflammation of a vertebra.

spondylolisthesis A back disease in which the lowermost lumbar vertebra (usually) gradually slides down the sloping upper surface of the sacrum, carrying the entire upper spinal column along with it.

spondylolysis A defect of a vertebra: a crack across the rear of a vertebra in such a way that the rear portion is detached from the front.

spondylosis *See* degenerative arthritis.

stiff spine *See* ankylosing spondylitis.

swayback *See* lordosis.

T

thoracic An adjective that means pertaining to the chest.

thoracic vertebrae The twelve chest vertebrae.

V

vertebra Any one of the several dozen individual bones that collectively make up the backbone.

vertebral column *See* spinal column.

W

wear-and-tear arthritis *See* degenerative arthritis.

INDEX

ABOUT THE AUTHOR
AND ILLUSTRATOR

MARION STEINMANN was for over twenty years a member of the editorial staff of *Life* magazine, serving as an associate editor and a science writer. She has also written for other consumer and scientific publications. This is her third book.

Ms. Steinmann was born in Rochester, New York, and received her bachelor of science degree from Cornell University. She is married to a professor of political science at Temple University.

MARK ROSENTHAL is a free-lance artist whose illustrations have appeared in numerous books, national magazines and newspapers. Born in Miami, Florida, he attended Cooper Union School of Art and is a graduate of New York University. He lives in Brooklyn with his wife.